# Essential Brazilian Portuguese

Written by
Dulce Marcello

Edited by
Laura Riggio

LIVING LANGUAGE®

Published in the United States by Living Language, an imprint of Random House, Inc.

www.livinglanguage.com

Editor: Laura Riggio
Production Editor: Ciara Robinson
Production Manager: Tom Marshall
Interior Design: Sophie Chin
Illustrations: Sophie Chin
Audio Producer: Ok Hee Kolwitz

First Edition

ISBN: 978-0-307-97207-1

This book is available at special discounts for bulk purchases for sales promotions or premiums. Special editions, including personalized covers, excerpts of existing books, and corporate imprints, can be created in large quantities for special needs. For more information, write to Special Markets/ Premium Sales, 1745 Broadway, MD 3-1, New York, New York 10019 or e-mail specialmarkets@ randomhouse.com.
PRINTED IN THE UNITED STATES OF AMERICA
10 9 8 7 6 5

## Acknowledgments

Thanks to the Living Language team: Amanda D'Acierno, Christopher Warnasch, Suzanne McQuade, Laura Riggio, Erin Quirk, Heather Dalton, Amanda Munoz, Fabrizio LaRocca, Siobhan O'Hare, Sophie Chin, Pat Stango, Sue Daulton, Alison Skrabek, Ciara Robinson, Andrea McLin, and Tom Marshall.

Special thanks to our audio producer Ok Hee Kolwitz and her team of narrators: Tatiane Amnuar, Sonaria Curtis, Marcos Daniel Ferreira, Alex Mascarenhas, and Rene Ruiz.

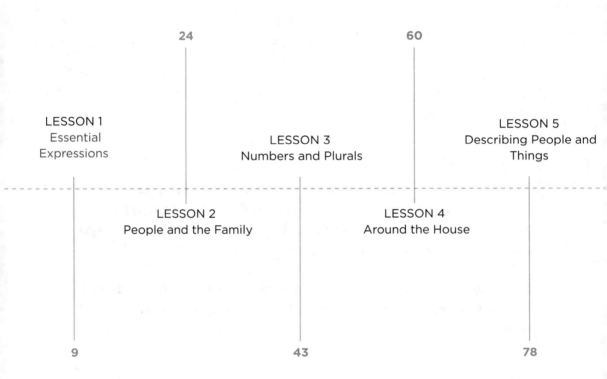

COURSE

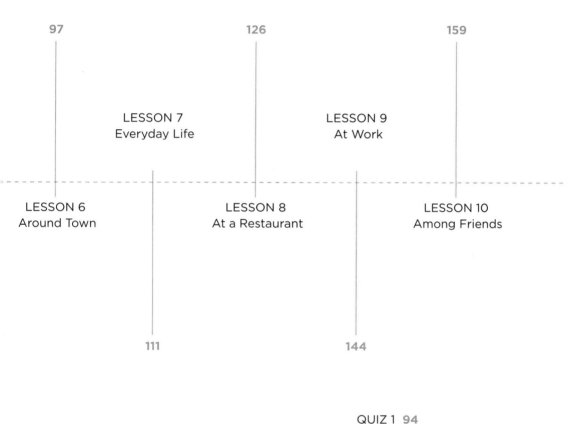

# How to Use This Course

Oi!

Welcome to *Living Language Essential Brazilian Portuguese*! Are you ready to learn how to speak, read, and write Portuguese?

Before we begin, let's go over what you'll see in this course. It's very easy to use, but this section will help you get started.

## LESSONS

There are 10 lessons in this course. Each lesson is divided into three parts and has the following components:

### PART 1

• **Vocabulary Builder 1** listing the key words and phrases for that lesson.

• **Vocabulary Practice 1** to practice what you learned in Vocabulary Builder 1.

• **Grammar Builder 1** to guide you through the structure of the Portuguese language (how to form sentences, questions, and so on).

### PART 2

• **Vocabulary Builder 2** listing more key words and phrases.

• **Vocabulary Practice 2** to practice what you learned in Vocabulary Builder 2.

• **Grammar Builder 2** for more information on language structure.

• **Work Out 1** for a comprehensive practice of what you've learned so far.

### PART 3

• **Bring It All Together** to put what you've learned in a conversational context through a dialogue, monologue, description, or other similar text.

• **Work Out 2** for another helpful practice exercise.

- **Drive It Home** to ingrain an important point of Portuguese structure for the long term.

- **Parting Words** outlining what you learned in the lesson.

## TAKE IT FURTHER

**Take It Further** sections scattered throughout the lesson to provide extra information about the new vocabulary you just saw, expand on grammar points, or introduce additional words and phrases.

## WORD RECALL

**Word Recall** sections appear in-between lessons. They review important vocabulary and grammar from previous lessons, including the one you just finished. These sections will reinforce what you've learned so far in the course, and help you retain the information for the long term.

## QUIZZES

This course contains two quizzes: **Quiz 1** is halfway through the course (after Lesson 5), and **Quiz 2** appears after the last lesson (Lesson 10). The quizzes are self-graded so it will be easy for you to test your progress and see if you need to go back and review once again.

## REVIEW DIALOGUES

There are five **Review Dialogues** at the end of the course, after Quiz 2. These everyday dialogues review what you learned in Lessons 1-10, introduce new vocabulary and structures, and allow you to become more familiar with conversational Portuguese. Each dialogue is followed by comprehension questions that serve as the course's final review.

## PROGRESS BAR

You will see a **Progress Bar** on almost every page that has course material. It indicates your current position in the course and lets you know how much progress you've made. Each line in the bar represents a lesson; the final line represents the Review Dialogues.

## AUDIO

Look for this symbol ▶ to help guide you through the audio as you read the book. It will tell you which track to listen to for each section. When you see the symbol, choose the track and start listening! If you don't see the symbol, then there isn't any audio for that section. The audio can be used on its own—in other words, without the book—when you're on the go. Whether in your car or at the gym, you can listen to the audio to brush up on your pronunciation and review what you've learned in the book.

## PRONUNCIATION GUIDE AND GRAMMAR SUMMARY

At the back of this book you will find a **Pronunciation Guide** and **Grammar Summary**. The Pronunciation Guide provides information on Portuguese pronunciation and the Grammar Summary contains a brief and helpful overview of Portuguese grammar.

## FREE ONLINE TOOLS

Go to **www.livinglanguage.com/languagelab** to access your free online tools. The tools are organized around the lessons in this course, together with audiovisual flashcards, and interactive games and quizzes. These tools will help you review and practice the vocabulary and grammar you have seen in the lessons, as well as provide extra words and phrases related to the lesson's topic.

# Lesson 1: Essential Expressions

**Lição Um: Expressões Essenciais**

**Bem-vindos!** *Welcome!* In this lesson, you'll learn some basic expressions and other useful words and phrases to get you started speaking Portuguese. You'll learn how to:

☐ greet people at different times of the day

☐ address someone formally and informally

☐ introduce yourself and say your name

☐ ask other people's names and find out how they're doing

☐ put it all together in a simple conversation

Let's get started with some basic vocabulary. **Prontos?** *Ready?*

Remember to look for this symbol ⊙ to help guide you through the audio as you read the book. For each section that has audio, it will tell you which track you should listen to. When you see the symbol, choose the track and start listening! If you don't see the symbol, then there isn't audio material for that section.

Essential Expressions          Numbers and Plurals          Describing People
                                                                 and Things
----------|-------------------|---------------------------|-----------|------

          People and the Family              Around the House

## Vocabulary Builder 1

⏵ 1A Vocabulary Builder 1 (CD: 1, Track: 2)

| | |
|---|---|
| *hi* | oi |
| *good morning* | bom dia |
| *good afternoon* | boa tarde |
| *good evening/good night* | boa noite |
| *How's it going? (infml.)* | Tudo bem? |
| *I'm fine. (infml.)* | Tudo bem. |
| *How are you? (fml.)* | Como vai? |
| *I'm fine. (fml.)* | Estou bem. |
| *And you?* | E você? |
| *thank you (m./f.)* | obrigado/a |
| *you're welcome* | de nada |
| *please* | por favor |
| *good-bye (fml.)* | até logo |
| *good-bye (infml.)* | tchau |
| *yes* | sim |
| *no* | não |

Note: The following abbreviations will be used in this course: (m.) = *masculine*, (f.) = *feminine*, (sg.)
= *singular*, (pl.) = *plural*, (fml.) = *formal*, (infml.) = *informal*, (lit.) = *literally*

## ✎ Vocabulary Practice 1

Let's practice the new vocabulary you've just learned! Match the Portuguese in
the left column with the English equivalent in the right.

1. oi                             a. *I'm fine (infml.)*

2. bom dia                        b. *And you?*

3. tchau                          c. *please*

| | |
|---|---|
| 4. boa tarde | d. *good-bye (infml.)* |
| 5. Como vai? | e. *good morning* |
| 6. E você? | f. *you're welcome* |
| 7. por favor | g. *How are you? (fml.)* |
| 8. tudo bem | h. *good evening/good night* |
| 9. boa noite | i. *hi* |
| 10. de nada | j. *good afternoon* |

**ANSWER KEY**
1. i; 2. e; 3. d; 4. j; 5. g; 6. b; 7. c; 8. a; 9. h; 10. f

## Take It Further

▶ 1B Take It Further (CD: 1, Track:3)

### PRONUNCIATION AND SPECIAL SYMBOLS

You've probably noticed that some words in Portuguese use special orthographic symbols or accents. Look at the table below that contains diacritic accents and practice pronouncing the words out loud to become familiar with the sounds.

| ACCENT | PURPOSE | EXAMPLE | SOUND IN ENGLISH |
|---|---|---|---|
| ~ til (tilde) | to produce a nasal vowel sound | não (*no*) | similar to the *ou* in *bound* |
| | | aviões (*airplanes*) | like the *o* in *don't*, followed by the *e* in *get* |
| | | mãe (*mother*) | like the *u* in *thunder*, followed by the *e* in *get* |

| ACCENT | PURPOSE | EXAMPLE | SOUND IN ENGLISH |
|---|---|---|---|
| ´ agudo (acute) | to show that the stress falls on that syllable in the case of e and o to mark an open vowel | café (coffee) | like the e in best |
| | | nós (we) | like the o in off (northeastern U.S. pronunciation) |
| | | possível (possible) | like the i in routine |
| ^ circunflexo (circumflex) | used to show that a vowel is stressed and closed | você (you) | like the ay in day but clipped |
| | | avô (grandfather) | like the o in go but clipped |
| ` grave (grave) | used to differentiate the grammatical category of certain words | a (the) à (to the) | no change in sound |
| ¸ cedilha (cedilla) | used on the c before a, o and u to indicate to sound s | açúcar (sugar) | sounds like the s in see notice that the second c is pronounced like the k in kite |

## Grammar Builder 1

▶ 1C Grammar Builder 1 (CD: 1, Track: 4)

### GREETINGS

Did you notice that the word obrigado/a (thank you) has two different endings? In Portuguese, nouns and adjectives have gender—meaning they can be masculine or feminine and can agree with what they are referring to. Just keep this in mind for now; you'll learn more about this in Lesson Two.

When asking *How are you?*, Portuguese uses the pronoun você (*you*) when speaking to both males and females. It's also used to address people informally, like family and friends. If you want to make speech more formal, replace the pronoun você (*you*) with the term o senhor (*sir*) or a senhora (*ma'am*) based on the gender of the person you are addressing.

Take a look at these examples:

| | |
|---|---|
| *How are you?* | Como vai você? (*infml.*) |
| | Como vai o senhor? (*fml./m.*) |
| | Como vai a senhora? (*fml./f.*) |
| *I'm fine, and you?* | Tudo bem, e você? (*infml.*) |
| | Estou bem, e o senhor? (*fml./m.*) |
| | Estou bem, e a senhora? (*fml./f.*) |

# Vocabulary Builder 2

▷ 1D Vocabulary Builder 2 (CD: 1, Track:5)

| | |
|---|---|
| *Excuse me.* | Com licença. |
| *I'm sorry.* | Desculpe. |
| *What's happening?* | E aí? |
| *What's your name?* (*infml.*) | Como você se chama? |
| *What's your name?* (*fml./m.*) | Como o senhor se chama? |
| *What's your name?* (*fml./f.*) | Como a senhora se chama? |
| *My name is …* | Eu me chamo … |
| *I'd like to introduce …* | Gostaria de apresentar … |
| *I'd like to introduce … to you.* | Quero lhe apresentar … |

| It's a pleasure. | Muito prazer. |
| The pleasure is mine. | O prazer é meu. |
| Do you speak English? (infml.) | Você fala inglês? |
| Do you speak English? (fml./m.) | O senhor fala inglês? |
| Do you speak English? (fml./f.) | A senhora fala inglês? |
| I don't speak Portuguese. | Eu não falo português. |
| Could you repeat? | Você poderia repetir? |
| I didn't understand. | Eu não entendi. |

# ✎ Vocabulary Practice 2

Translate the following phrases into English. Feel free to use a dictionary if you need to.

1. Com licença. _____

2. Desculpe. _____

3. Como você se chama? _____

4. Eu me chamo … _____

5. Gostaria de apresentar … _____

6. Quero lhe apresentar … _____

7. Muito prazer. _____

8. O prazer é meu. _____

9. Você fala inglês? _____

10. Eu não falo português. _____

## Take it Further

▶ 1E Take It Further (CD: 1, Track: 6)

### PRONUNCIATION: M AND N

The consonants m and n either at the end or in the middle of a word before a consonant are used to nasalize the preceding vowel, and aren't really pronounced on their own.

So in ponte (*bridge*) the n makes the o sound nasal, like the *on* in *don't*.

Likewise, in the word cama (*bed*), the first a has the nasal sound like the *un* in *bunch*, but note that the second a is not nasalized and sounds like the *a* in *father*.

However, when a word ends with an m, the m is pronounced as an n. Keep in mind that the preceding vowel is still nasalized as in examples above. So the om in bom (*good*) sounds like the English *on* in *don't*.

Be careful. If there is an n or m between two vowels, the m or n forms a syllable with the second vowel, meaning that the first vowel isn't nasalized. Compare the following pairs of words, in which the first one has a nasal vowel, and the second one doesn't:

limpa (*clean*)/lima (*lime*)

grande (*big*)/grana (*money-infml*)

Finally, when a word starts with an m, like mala (*suitcase*), the m sounds like the English *m* in Mary. The same goes for words that start with an n, like nada (*nothing*), the n sounds like the *n* in *nest*.

---

# Grammar Builder 2
▶ 1F Grammar Builder 2 (CD: 1, Track: 7)

## MORE ON GREETINGS

In Vocabulary Builder 2 you saw the sentence: Você fala inglês (*You speak English*). You can make this sentence formal and masculine: O senhor fala inglês, or formal and feminine: A senhora fala inglês.

Placing the masculine senhor or the feminine senhora before a person's last name has the same function as the English Mr. or Mrs./Ms., although it is perceived the highest level of formality in Brazil. In writing, use the abbreviated form, Sr. (*Mr.*); or Sra. (*Mrs./Ms.*).

In Brazil, it is common practice to also use a person's first name with senhor or senhora in formal situations. Senhor can be abbreviated to Seu as in Seu Agenor while Senhora can also be realized as Dona such as Dona Maria.

Informal:
Você fala português, Paulo?
*Do you speak Portuguese, Paul?*

Formal:
O senhor fala português, Sr. Paulo?
*Do you speak Portuguese, Mr. Paul?*

Very formal:

O senhor fala português, Sr. Smith?

*Do you speak Portuguese, Mr. Smith?*

Here are some more formal and informal greetings and essential expressions.

| | |
|---|---|
| *How's everything?* | Tudo certo? |
| *See you later.* | Até mais tarde. |
| *Come in, please.* | Entre, por favor. |
| *Thank you very much. (fml./m.)* | Muito obrigado. |
| *Thank you very much. (fml/f.)* | Muito obrigada. |
| *Don't mention it.* | Não há de que. |
| *Please (infml)* | Faça o favor. |
| *Do me a favor.* | Faça-me um favor. |
| *Can you help me?* | Você pode me ajudar? |
| *Could you help me? (fml./m.)* | O senhor poderia me ajudar? |
| *Could you help me? (fml./f.)* | A senhora poderia me ajudar? |
| *Help!* | Socorro! |

Note the difference between Você pode me ajudar? (*Can you help me?*), which is used to ask for a favor, and Socorro! (*Help!*), which is used in an emergency.

Also notice the difference between faça-me um favor (*do me a favor*) when asking for favors, and faça o favor which is an informal expression used to soften requests or commands.

Abra a janela, faça o favor.

*Open the window, will you?*

## ✎ Work Out 1

Complete the following sentences with the correct word from the list below.

bem, como, muito, prazer, até, vai, ajudar, licença, fala, entendi

1. _____ vai?

   *How are you?*

2. _____ logo.

   *Good-bye.*

3. Como _____ a senhora?

   *How are you, ma'am?*

4. Estou _____, e o senhor?

   *I'm fine, and you (fml.)?*

5. Com _____.

   *Excuse me.*

6. Muito _____.

   *It's a pleasure.*

7. Você _____ inglês?

   *Do you speak English?*

8. Eu não _____.

   *I didn't understand.*

9. Você pode me _____?

   *Can you help me?*

10. _____ obrigado.

*Thank you very much.*

**ANSWER KEY**

1. Como; 2. Até; 3. vai; 4. bem; 5. licença; 6. prazer; 7. fala; 8. entendi; 9. ajudar; 10. Muito

# 🔊 Bring It All Together

▶ 1G Bring It All Together (CD: 1, Track: 8)

Now let's bring it all together, and add a little bit more vocabulary and structure.

| | |
|---|---|
| *Sandra:* | *Hi, Gustavo. What's happening?* |
| Sandra: | Oi, Gustavo. E aí? |
| *Gustavo:* | *Hi, Sandra. I'm fine.* |
| Gustavo: | Oi, Sandra. Tudo bem. |
| *Sandra:* | *This is Jane.* |
| Sandra: | Esta é a Jane. |
| *Gustavo:* | *Hi, Jane. It's a pleasure.* |
| Gustavo: | Oi, Jane. Prazer. |
| *Jane:* | *It's a pleasure, Gustavo.* |
| Jane: | Prazer, Gustavo. |
| *Gustavo:* | *Are you American?* |
| Gustavo: | Você é americana? |
| *Jane:* | *No, I'm Australian.* |
| Jane: | Não, eu sou australiana. |
| *Gustavo:* | *Welcome to Brazil!* |
| Gustavo: | Bem-vinda ao Brasil! |
| *Jane:* | *Cool!* |
| Jane: | Legal! |

## ✎ Work Out 2

The dialogue you heard in Bring It All Together is informal. Below is a version of what a formal dialogue would look like. Complete the dialogue below with the correct words from the list.

vindo, bem, obrigado, senhor, vai, não, quero, prazer

1. Sra. Dias: Como _____ o senhor, Sr. Morais?

   *How are you, Mr. Morais?*

2. Sr. Morais: Estou _____, Sra. Dias. E a senhora?

   *I'm fine, Mrs. Dias, and you?*

3. Sra. Dias: Estou bem. _____ lhe apresentar o Sr. Smith.

   *I'm fine. I'd like to introduce you to Mr. Smith.*

4. Sr. Smith: Muito _____, Sr. Morais.

   *It's a pleasure.*

5. Sr. Morais: O prazer é meu. O _____ é americano?

   *The pleasure is mine. Are you American?*

6. Sr. Smith: _____, eu sou australiano.

   *No, I'm Australian.*

7. Sr. Morais: Bem-_____ ao Brasil!

   *Welcome to Brazil.*

8. Sr. Smith: Muito _____.

   *Thank you very much.*

**ANSWER KEY**
1. vai; 2. bem; 3. Quero; 4. prazer; 5. senhor; 6. Não; 7. vindo; 8. obrigado

# ✎ Drive It Home

Read the following scenarios and respond in Portuguese.

1. Greet a friend in the morning and ask him/her if everything is fine.

2. Greet an elderly neighbor in the evening and ask her how she is.

3. Introduce Rita, a colleague at work, to Mr. Silva, and tell her that Mr. Silva is Brazilian.

4. Introduce Antônio, a friend, to another friend, Sandra.

5. Greet an elderly woman in the afternoon and ask her name.

6. Say thank you and good-bye to a salesman at a shop.

7. Apologize, say you didn't understand, and then ask a gentleman to repeat.

8. Say excuse me, ask a stranger if she speaks English and then tell her you don't speak Portuguese.

**ANSWER KEY**

1. Bom dia, tudo bem? 2. Boa noite, como vai a senhora? 3. Sr. Silva, quero lhe apresentar Rita. Rita, Sr. Silva é brasileiro. 4. Antônio, gostaria de lhe apresentar Sandra. 5. Boa tarde. Como a senhora

se chama? **6.** Muito obrigado/muito obrigada. Até logo. **7.** Desculpe, eu não entendi. O senhor poderia repetir? **8.** Com licença, a senhora fala inglês? Eu não falo português.

# Parting Words

**Muito bem!** *Well done!* You just finished your first lesson of Essential Brazilian Portuguese! How did you do? You should now be able to:

☐ greet people at different times of the day (Still unsure? Go back to page 10.)

☐ address someone formally and informally (Still unsure? Go back to page 12.)

☐ introduce yourself and say your name (Still unsure? Go back to page 13.)

☐ ask other people's names and find out how they're doing (Still unsure? Go back to page 16.)

☐ put it all together in a simple conversation (Still unsure? Go back to page 19.)

Don't forget to practice and reinforce what you've learned by visiting www.livinglanguage.com/languagelab for flashcards, games, and quizzes!

# Take It Further

▶ 1H Take It Further (CD: 1, Track: 9)

Now that you speak a little Portuguese, it's time to practice saying that along with a few other expressions.

| I speak a little Portuguese. | Eu falo um pouco de português. |
|---|---|
| I'm learning Portuguese. | Estou aprendendo português. |
| Speak more slowly. | Fale mais devagar. |
| Congratulations! | Parabéns! |
| Very good! | Muito bem! |

# Word Recall

You will see this section between each lesson. It gives you the chance to review key vocabulary from all of the previous lessons up to that point, not only the lesson you've just completed. This will reinforce the vocabulary as well as some of the structures that you've learned so far in the course in order for you to retain them in your long-term memory. For now, though, we'll only review the key vocabulary you learned in Lesson One.

How would you answer these remarks in Portuguese? In some cases, there can be more than one correct answer.

1. Obrigada. _____

2. Você é brasileiro? _____

3. Como vai? _____

4. Até logo. _____

5. Você fala português? _____

6. Gostaria de lhe apresentar a Sra. Medeiros. _____

7. Como você se chama? _____

8. Parabéns! _____

**ANSWER KEY**
1. De nada. 2. Não, eu sou … 3. Tudo bem. 4. Até logo. 5. Sim, eu falo um pouco de português./Sim, estou aprendendo português. 6. Muito prazer, Sra. Medeiros. 7. Eu me chamo … 8. Obrigado/obrigada.

# Lesson 2: People and the Family

## Lição Dois: Pessoas e Família

Oi! *Hi!* In your second lesson, you'll learn how to talk about people and members of your family. You'll also continue to learn key structures in Portuguese. By the end of this lesson, you'll be able to:

☐ talk about members of your family

☐ use definite articles (*the*)

☐ talk about people

☐ use *there is* and *there are* in Portuguese

☐ use what you've learned to tell someone about your family.

Let's start with some vocabulary. Vamos lá! *Let's go!*

# Vocabulary Builder 1

▶ 2A Vocabulary Builder 1 (CD: 1, Track: 10)

| | |
|---|---|
| mother | mãe |
| father | pai |
| brother | irmão |
| sister | irmã |
| teacher (m./f.) | professor/professora |
| student | estudante |
| man | homem |
| woman | mulher |
| husband | marido |
| wife | mulher |
| friend (m./f.) | amigo/amiga |
| boy | menino |
| girl | menina |
| person | pessoa |
| house | casa |
| office | escritório |
| doctor (m./f.) | médico/médica |
| daughter | filha |
| son | filho |

Note: In Portuguese the word for *wife* is the same as the word for *woman*: mulher. There's also the more formal term esposa (*wife*) and esposo (*husband*).

# ✎ Vocabulary Practice 1

Translate the following words into Portuguese.

1. *office* _____

2. *sister* _____

3. *house* _____

4. *mother* _____

5. *father* _____

6. *man* _____

7. *woman* _____

8. *student* _____

9. *teacher (m.)* _____

10. *girl* _____

11. *daughter* _____

12. *boy* _____

13. *person* _____

14. *friend* _____

**ANSWER KEY**
1. escritório; 2. irmã; 3. casa; 4. mãe; 5. pai; 6. homem; 7. mulher; 8. estudante; 9. professor; 10. menina; 11. filha; 12. menino; 13. pessoa; 14. amigo

## Take It Further

▶ 2B Take It Further (CD: 1, Track: 11)

### PRONOUNCING CONSONANTS 1

In Vocabulary Builder 1 you learned the words mulher (*woman*) and filha (*daughter*). Below is a small chart to help you pronounce the combination of these two consonants which is very common in Portuguese.

| lh | like the *lli* in *million* | filho (*son*), milho (*corn*) |
|----|------------------------------|-------------------------------|
| nh | like the *ni* in *onion* | espanhol (*Spanish*), tenho (*I have*) |

Here are some other examples:

O homem de Ilhéus.
*The man from Ilheus.*

Manhattan é uma ilha.
*Manhattan is an island.*

Não há nenhum.
*There isn't any.*

## Grammar Builder 1

▶ 2C Grammar Builder 1 (CD: 1, Track: 12)

### THE DEFINITE ARTICLES A AND O

As you know, a noun refers to a person, place or thing. While very few English nouns have a feminine or masculine form, for example *host/hostess*, all nouns in Portuguese have a grammatical gender.

The definite article, *the*, which in Portuguese is o for the masculine article and a for the feminine, reflects the gender of a noun. Look at the following examples:

|  | MASCULINE | FEMININE |
|---|---|---|
| *the neighbor* | o vizinho | a vizinha |
| *the cousin* | o primo | a prima |
| *the Brazilian* | o brasileiro | a brasileira |
| *the American* | o americano | a americana |
| *the nurse* | o enfermeiro | a enfermeira |

The list above contains nouns that refer to people. Other nouns that refer to places or things are also either masculine or feminine.

| *the house* | a casa |
|---|---|
| *the apartment* | o apartamento |
| *the water* | a água |
| *the beach* | a praia |
| *the watch/the clock* | o relógio |
| *the street* | a rua |
| *the (drinking) glass* | o copo |
| *the table* | a mesa |
| *the book* | o livro |

You'll notice that the nouns above end in either o or a, but not all nouns have these endings. Take a look at these examples:

| *the coffee* | o café |
|---|---|
| *the sugar* | o açúcar |
| *the chalk* | o giz |
| *the man* | o homem |
| *the restaurant* | o restaurante |
| *the ring* | o anel |

| the engine | o motor |
| the evening/night | a noite |

The definite articles o and a, which are used much more often than *the* in English, will always tell you the gender of the noun. When you learn new vocabulary, you should learn each noun with its corresponding article.

## Take it Further

▶ 2D Take It Further (CD: 1, Track: 13)

### NUMBERS 1 AND 2

| one (m.) | um |
| one (f.) | uma |
| two (m.) | dois |
| two (f.) | duas |

In Portuguese, the numbers *one* and *two* can be either masculine or feminine, so they agree in gender with the noun they're referring to. You'll learn more about numbers in the next lesson but for now, let's take a look at a few examples:

| one male cousin | um primo |
| one female cousin | uma prima |
| two bedrooms | dois quartos |
| two suitcases | duas malas |

# Vocabulary Builder 2

▷ 2E Vocbulary Builder 2  (CD: 1, Track: 14)

| the best friend (m.) | o melhor amigo |
|---|---|
| the grandfather | o avô |
| the grandmother | a avó |
| father-in-law | sogro |
| mother-in-law | sogra |
| brother-in-law | cunhado |
| sister-in-law | cunhada |
| son-in-law | genro |
| daughter-in-law | nora |
| stepson | enteado |
| daughter | enteada |
| stepfather | padrasto |
| stepmother | madrasta |
| the colleague (m./f.) | o/a colega |
| the manager (m./f.) | o/a gerente |
| the cell phone | o telefone celular |
| the email | o correio eletrônico |
| the postcard | o cartão postal |
| the receptionist (m./f.) | o/a recepcionista |
| the uncle and the aunt | o tio e a tia |
| the name | o nome |
| the last name | o sobrenome |

# Take It Further

▶ 2F Take It Further (CD: 1, Track: 15)

## PRONOUNCING CONSONANTS 2

Let's look at how to pronounce more consonants in Portuguese.

| c | before a, o, u and consonants other than h, like the *k* in *kite* | caro (*expensive*), capital (*capital*) |
|---|---|---|
| c | before e and i, like the *c* in *center* | cidade (*city*), especial (*special*) |
| h | silent | hotel (*hotel*) |
| l | usually close to the *l* in *lead*, but with the tongue further forward on the roof of the mouth | lavar (*to wash*), dólar (*dollar*) |
| l | at the end of a word, softened, similar to the *w* in *we* | final (*final*), Brasil (*Brazil*) |

Remember that when you say hotel in Portuguese, you're actually going to say [OH-tew].

Here are some other common words that start with a silent h: hora (*hour*), honesto (*honest*), and honrar (*to honor*).

# ✎ Vocabulary Practice 2

Give the correct definite article: o or a.

1. _____ copo

   *the glass*

2. _____ professor

   *the teacher (m.)*

3. _____ casa

   *the house*

4. _____ irmão

   *the brother*

5. _____ menina

   *the girl*

6. _____ amigo

   *the friend (m.)*

7. _____ água

   *the water*

8. _____ mulher

   *the woman*

9. _____ restaurante

   *the restaurant*

10. _____ dia

    *the day*

11. _____ brasileira

    *the Brazilian woman*

12. _____ lápis

    *the pencil*

13. _____ homem

    *the man*

14. _____ pai

    *the father*

15. _____ marido

    *the husband*

**ANSWER KEY**
1. o; 2. o; 3. a; 4. o; 5. a; 6. o; 7. a; 8. a; 9. o; 10. o; 11. a; 12. o; 13. o; 14. o; 15. o

# Grammar Builder 2
▶ 2G Grammar Builder 2 (CD: 1, Track: 16)

## HÁ (*THERE IS/THERE ARE*)

Há means both *there is* and *there are*.

Há uma casa.
*There is a house.*

Há um menino.
*There is a boy.*

**Há dois carros.**
*There are two cars.*

**Há duas professoras.**
*There are two teachers.*

To make a sentence negative, use não (*no*) before há.

**Não há um quarto.**
*There isn't a bedroom.*

**Não há dois copos.**
*There aren't two glasses.*

To form a question when writing, just place a question mark at the end of a written sentence. You will learn more about how to form questions in later lessons. For now, note that there's no word inversion, such as in English when you ask a question (*Is there? /Are there?*). The intonation, with a slight rise in the pitch toward the end of the sentence, will indicate to the listener that it is a question and not a statement.

**Há um médico?**
*Is there a doctor?*

## HERE AND THERE

Use aqui and ali to say *here* and *there*.

**Há um professor aqui e três estudantes ali.**
*There is a teacher here and three students there.*

Portuguese uses lá to indicate *over there*.

Há um bom hotel lá.

*There's a good hotel over there.*

## Take it Further

▶ 2H Take It Further (CD: 1, Track: 17)

Here are a few essential words and expressions to increase your vocabulary.

| | |
|---|---|
| *and* | e |
| *too* | também |
| *of course* | é claro |
| *is* | é |
| *several* | vários (*m.*)/várias (*f.*) |

## ✎ Work Out 1

Complete the following sentences with the correct word from the list below. Use the translation to guide you.

jornal, estudante, duas, dois, professora, amigos, homem, americana

1. Há um _____.

   *There's a student.*

2. Há uma _____.

   *There's a teacher.*

3. Não há _____ amigos.

   *There aren't two friends.*

4. Há dois _____.

*There are two friends.*

5. Há _____ mulheres.

*There are two women.*

6. Há um _____.

*There's a man.*

7. Há uma _____.

*There's an American woman.*

8. Não há um _____.

*There isn't a newspaper.*

**ANSWER KEY**
1. estudante; 2. professora; 3. dois; 4. amigos; 5. duas; 6. homem; 7. americana; 8. jornal

## Bring It All Together

2I Bring It All Together (CD: 1, Track: 18)

Now let's bring it all together, and add a little bit more vocabulary and structure with this monologue.

*My family.*
**A minha família.**

*I want to introduce my family.*
**Quero apresentar a minha família.**

*In my family, there's a father, Mr. Carlos.*
**Na minha família há um pai, o Sr. Carlos.**

*There's a mother, Mrs. Ana.*
Há uma mãe, a Sra. Ana.

*There's a brother, Pedro, a teacher.*
Há um irmão, Pedro, professor.

*And there's a sister, Sonia, a doctor.*
E há uma irmã, Sônia, médica.

*There are two grandfathers and two grandmothers.*
Há dois avôs e duas avós.

*There are aunts, uncles, and cousins.*
Há tios, tias, primos e primas.

*There's also Juca. Juca is the dog!*
Também há o Juca. O Juca é o cachorro!

## ✎ Work Out 2

Complete the phrases below with the correct noun in the feminine or masculine. The article and the translation will help you. Remember to repeat the sentence orally after it's complete.

1. a _____

   *the wife*

2. a _____

   *the teacher*

3. a _____

   *the friend*

4. o _____

   *the cousin*

5. o _____

   *the doctor*

6. o _____

   *the grandfather*

7. a _____

   *the American*

8. o _____

   *the son*

**ANSWER KEY**
1. **mulher/esposa**; 2. **professora**; 3. **amiga**; 4. **primo**; 5. **médico**; 6. **avô**; 7. **americana**; 8. **filho**

# Take It Further
▶ 2J Take It Further (CD: 1, Track: 19)

## PRONOUNCING CONSONANTS 3

| t | before a, o, u and other consonants like the *t* in *take* | tarde *(afternoon)*, todo *(all)* |
|---|---|---|
| t | before e and i, like the *ch* in *choose* | tia *(aunt)*, importante *(important)* |

As with other consonants, the consonant t may sound different depending on the region you go to in Brazil. In the south, people from the states of Paraná, Santa Catarina and Rio Grande do Sul tend to pronounce the t as it is spelled even when followed by e or i; while people from the states of Rio de Janeiro and São Paulo tend to pronounce the t followed by e or i as a *ch*, like in the examples above.

So in Paraná, dente (*tooth*) is [DEN-te], while in São Paulo, it's pronounced [DEN-chee].

Note that regional pronunciations do not drastically alter the sounds of words. Remember that this happens when Americans and British speakers pronounce their *t* as well!

---

## ✎ Drive it Home

Give the feminine of the following nouns. Be sure to add the article a.

1. o primo     _____

   *the cousin*

2. o professor     _____

   *the teacher*

3. o americano     _____

   *the American*

4. o homem     _____

   *the man*

5. o filho _____

   *the son*

6. o estudante _____

   *the student*

7. o amigo _____

   *the friend*

8. o pai _____

   *the father*

9. o avô _____

   *the grandfather*

10. o colega _____

    *the colleague*

11. o médico _____

    *the doctor*

12. o enfermeiro _____

    *the nurse*

13. o marido _____

    *the husband*

14. o turista _____

    *the tourist*

15. o recepcionista _____

    *the receptionist*

**ANSWER KEY**

1. a prima; 2. a professora; 3. a americana; 4. a mulher; 5. a filha; 6. a estudante; 7. a amiga; 8. a mãe; 9. a avó; 10. a colega; 11. a médica; 12. a enfermeira; 13. a mulher/esposa; 14. a turista; 15. a recepcionista

# Parting Words

Parabéns! *Congratulations!* You finished the lesson! How did you do? You should now be able to:

☐ talk about members of your family (Still unsure? Go back to page 25.)

☐ use definite articles (*the*) (Still unsure? Go back to page 27.)

☐ talk about people (Still unsure? Go back to page 30.)

☐ use *there is* and *there are* in Portuguese (Still unsure? Go back to page 33.)

☐ use what you've learned to tell someone about your family (Still unsure? Go back to page 36.)

Don't forget to practice and reinforce what you've learned by visiting www.livinglanguage.com/languagelab for flashcards, games, and quizzes!

# Word Recall

Translate the following words and phrases into Portuguese.

1. *yes/no* _____

2. *sister* _____

3. *uncle's wife* _____

4. *please* _____

5. *sister's husband* _____

6. *and* _____

7. *too* _____

8. *aunt's son* _____

9. *excuse me* _____

10. *mother's mother* _____

**ANSWER KEY**
1. sim/não; 2. a irmã; 3. a tia; 4. por favor; 5. o cunhado 6. e; 7. também; 8. o primo; 9. com licença; 10. a avó

Essential Brazilian Portuguese

# Lesson 3: Numbers and Plurals

**Lição Três: Números e Plurais**

**Oi!** *Hi!* In this lesson, you'll learn how to:

☐ count

☐ use *a/an* and *some*

☐ form plurals in Portuguese

☐ use the verb **ter** (*to have*)

☐ put it all together in a short conversation

**Adiante!** (*Go) ahead!*

## Vocabulary Builder 1

▶ 3A Vocabulary Builder 1 (CD: 1, Track: 20)

| | |
|---|---|
| one (m.) | um |
| one (f.) | uma |
| two (m.) | dois |
| two (f.) | duas |
| three | três |
| four | quatro |
| five | cinco |
| six | seis |
| seven | sete |
| eight | oito |
| nine | nove |
| ten | dez |
| eleven | onze |
| twelve | doze |
| thirteen | treze |
| fourteen | quatorze |
| fifteen | quinze |
| sixteen | dezesseis |
| seventeen | dezessete |
| eighteen | dezoito |
| nineteen | dezenove |
| twenty | vinte |

# ✎ Vocabulary Practice 1

Fill in the sentences below with the correct number using the translation to help you. Repeat the sentence out loud after it's complete for extra practice!

1. Há _____ turistas.

   *There are twenty tourists.*

2. Não há _____ mapas.

   *There aren't three maps.*

3. Há _____ gatos e _____ cães.

   *There are five cats and six dogs.*

4. Há _____ amigos e _____ amigas.

   *There are eight male friends and nine female friends.*

5. Há _____ xícaras lá?

   *Are there seven cups over there?*

6. Não há _____ rádios, há _____.

   *There aren't ten radios; there are eleven.*

7. Há _____ professores e _____ estudantes.

   *There are four teachers and fourteen students.*

8. Há _____ gerentes e _____ clientes.

   *There are two managers and twelve clients.*

9. Há _____ jornal e _____ revistas.

   *There is one newspaper and two magazines.*

10. Há _____ casas e _____ apartamentos.

*There are six houses and sixteen apartments.*

**ANSWER KEY**
1. vinte; 2. três; 3. cinco, seis; 4. oito, nove; 5. sete; 6. dez, onze; 7. quatro, quatorze; 8. dois, doze; 9. um, duas; 10. seis, dezesseis

# Grammar Builder 1
▶ 3B Grammar Builder 1 (CD: 1, Track: 21)

## INDEFINITE ARTICLES AND FORMING THE PLURAL

You already learned the definite articles o and a (*the*). Now let's look at the indefinite articles um and uma and how to use them.

| | |
|---|---|
| *a/an (m./sg.)* | um |
| *a/an (f./sg.)* | uma |
| *a man* | um homem |
| *a child* | uma criança |
| *an apple* | uma maçã |
| *an egg* | um ovo |

The plural forms of the indefinite article are equivalent to the English *some*.

| | |
|---|---|
| *some (m./pl.)* | uns |
| *some (f./pl.)* | umas |

The articles o and a (*the*) also have a plural form: os and as.

| | SINGULAR | PLURAL |
|---|---|---|
| *the book* | o livro | os livros |
| *the orange* | a laranja | as laranjas |

To form the plural of most nouns ending in a vowel, just add an s.

| | |
|---|---|
| *some keys* | umas chaves |
| *some monuments* | uns monumentos |
| *the cats* | os gatos |
| *the radios* | os rádios |
| *the cups* | as xícaras |
| *the clients* | os clientes |
| *the pens* | as canetas |
| *the magazines* | as revistas |
| *the ice-cream* | os sorvetes |
| *the tables* | as mesas |
| *the photographs* | as fotografias |

Not all nouns in Portuguese form their plural like this. For example, for words ending in –ão, there are three different plurals.

| | | |
|---|---|---|
| *the dog* | o cão | os cães |
| *the hand* | a mão | as mãos |
| *the airplane* | o avião | os aviões |

Words ending in –m change the –m to –ns.

| | | |
|---|---|---|
| *the man* | o homem | os homens |

Nouns ending in –r, –z, and –s add –es to form the plural.

| | | |
|---|---|---|
| *the doctor* | o doutor | os doutores |

And finally, words ending in –l drop the –l and add –is.

| | | |
|---|---|---|
| *the newspaper* | o jornal | os jornais |

# Take It Further

▶ 3C Take It Further  (CD: 1, Track: 22):

## PRONOUNCING S

Now that you've learned how to form plurals, let's see how the consonant s can be pronounced differently depending on where it's placed. Look at the chart below.

| s | at the beginning of a word or after another consonant, like the s in see | saco (bag), mensagem (message) |
|---|---|---|
| s | between vowels, like the z in zipper | rosa (rose), mesa (table) |
| s | before b, d, soft g (ge and gi), j, l, m, n, r, v, or z like the z in zipper | mesmo (same), esmeralda (emerald) |
| s | before hard c, hard g, f, p, q and t, and in final position, like the s in see | esposa (wife), destino (destiny), canetas (pens) |
| ss | like ss in message | classe (class), nosso (our) |

Note that the final s is pronounced like sh in Rio de Janeiro. For example, you'll probably hear the word canetas (pens) pronounced [ka-NEH-tash] in Rio, whereas you'll hear it pronounced [ka-NEH-tass] in São Paulo and most other regions of Brazil.

Listen to some Bossa Nova to see if you notice the final sh sound and practice pronouncing it just like the famous singers!

## Vocabulary Builder 2

▶ 3D Vocabulary Builder 2 (CD: 1, Track: 23)

| | |
|---|---|
| *I have homework.* | Eu tenho lição de casa. |
| *You have a headache.* | Você tem dor de cabeça. |
| *He has a backache.* | Ele tem dor nas costas. |
| *She has a toothache.* | Ela tem dor de dente. |
| *You have a beach house.* | Vocês têm uma casa de praia. |
| *They have several credit cards.* | Eles têm vários cartões de crédito. |
| *They have money.* | Elas têm dinheiro. |
| *She has five teachers.* | Ela tem cinco professores. |
| *You have ten airplanes.* | Vocês têm dez aviões. |
| *They have seven rings.* | Eles têm sete anéis. |

## Take It Further

▶ 3E Take It Further (CD: 1, Track: 24)

### WORD STRESS

Words ending in –a, –e, –o or the consonants –s, –m, or –ns are usually stressed on the penultimate (second-to-last) syllable:

gato (*cat*), homem (*man*), elefante (*elephant*), garagem (*garage*).

Words ending in –i, –u (or –i, –u followed by –m, or –s), or a diphthong*, including nasals (or a diphthong followed by –s), are stressed on the last syllable:

depois (*after*), aqui (*here*)

If a word does not follow one of the two rules above, a written accent marks the syllable that is stressed. The acute accent on í or ú simply marks stress, but on á, é, or ó it marks both stress and an open vowel. The circumflex on â, ê, and ô represents a closed vowel sound. The grave accent is only used over the letter à in certain contractions. It doesn't change the stress of a word.

fácil (*easy*), música (*music*), agradável (*pleasant*), automóvel (*automobile*), você (*you*), cônsul (*consul*), câmera (*camera*), às (*to*)

\* A diphthong is a combination of two vowels that make one sound together, like the long vowel sound in English. So the ei in seis (*six*) is pronounced like the *a* in *hate*.

---

## ✎ Vocabulary Practice 2

Complete the sentences below with the correct word or phrase.

1. Eu tenho vinte _____.

   *I have twenty books.*

2. Nós temos _____.

   *We have a beach house.*

3. Vocês têm _____.

   *You have homework.*

4. Elas têm dez _____.

   *They have ten photographs.*

5. Você tem _____.

   *You have money.*

6. **Ele tem quatro** _____.

   *He has four cats.*

7. **Eles têm** _____.

   *They have a headache.*

8. **Ela tem dois** _____.

   *She has two offices.*

9. **Maria e Pedro têm três** _____.

   *Maria and Pedro have three children.*

10. **Você e Aparecida têm** _____.

   *You and Aparecida have a car.*

**ANSWER KEY**

1. livros; 2. uma casa de praia; 3. lição de casa; 4. fotografias; 5. dinheiro; 6. gatos; 7. dor de cabeça; 8. escritórios; 9. filhos; 10. um carro

# Grammar Builder 2

▶ 3F Grammar Builder 2 (CD: 1, Track: 25)

## THE SUBJECT PRONOUN

| I | eu |
|---|---|
| you | você |
| he | ele |
| she | ela |
| we | nós |
| you (pl.) | vocês |
| they (m.) | eles |
| they (f.) | elas |

Note that the subject pronouns have both a feminine and a masculine form in the plural too: eles, elas (*they*). Portuguese does not have the subject pronoun *it*.

## THE VERB TER (*TO HAVE*)

The verb ter (*to have*) is irregular. Note that there's an accent mark on the second and third person plural, but that it does not change the pronunciation.

| *I have* | eu tenho |
| *you have* | você tem |
| *he has* | ele tem |
| *she has* | ela tem |
| *we have* | nós temos |
| *you have (pl.)* | vocês têm |
| *they have (m.)* | eles têm |
| *they have (f.)* | elas têm |

Now, let's look at some example sentences.

| *I have a daughter.* | Eu tenho uma filha. |
| *You have two dogs.* | Você tem dois cães. |
| *He has three books.* | Ele tem três livros. |
| *We have four children.* | Nós temos quatro filhos. |

In the sentence nós temos quatro filhos (*we have four children*) above, note that filhos can refer to four sons, or to sons and daughters.

Therefore, when you say nós temos amigas (*we have friends*), you're referring to a group of female friends. When you say nós temos amigos (*we have friends*), you're referring either to a group of male friends or to a mixed group of male and female friends.

## IDIOMATIC EXPRESSIONS WITH TER

Here are some common idiomatic expressions using the verb ter (*to have*). Note that it is used in many common expressions where English uses the verb *to be*.

| | |
|---|---|
| *to have luck* | ter sorte |
| *to have bad luck* | ter azar |
| *to have a problem* | ter um problema |
| *to be thirsty* | ter sede |
| *to be hungry* | ter fome |
| *to be sleepy* | ter sono |
| *to be afraid* | ter medo |
| *to have time* | ter tempo |
| *Have a nice day!* | Tenha um bom dia! |

# ✎ Work Out 1

Complete the following with the appropriate indefinite article and then translate.

1. _____ turista

2. _____ dia

3. _____ jornais

4. _____ professora

5. _____ pessoas

6. _____ amigos

7. _____ escritórios

8. _____ anéis

9. _____ canetas

10. _____ cartão de crédito

**ANSWER KEY**

1. um/uma (*a tourist*); 2. um (*a day*); 3. uns (*some newspapers*); 4. uma (*a teacher*); 5. umas (*some people*); 6. uns (*some friends*); 7. uns (*some offices*); 8. uns (*some rings*); 9. umas (*some pens*); 10. um (*a credit card*)

# Bring It All Together

▶ 3G Bring It All Together (CD: 1, Track: 26)

Now let's bring it all together and add a little bit more vocabulary and structure. Read and listen to the following dialogue between two friends.

| | |
|---|---|
| *Paulo:* | *Hi Sandra! How's everything?* |
| Paulo: | Oi Sandra! Tudo bem? |
| *Sandra:* | *Fine. Let's play tennis?* |
| Sandra: | Tudo bem. Vamos jogar tênis? |
| *Paulo:* | *I have two racquets.* |
| Paulo: | Eu tenho duas raquetes. |
| *Sandra:* | *Great! I have some balls.* |
| Sandra: | Ótimo! Eu tenho umas bolas. |
| *Paulo:* | *Do you have an aspirin? I have a headache.* |
| Paulo: | Você tem uma aspirina? Eu tenho dor de cabeça. |
| *Sandra:* | *No, I don't have an aspirin. Sorry.* |
| Sandra: | Não, eu não tenho aspirina. Sinto muito. |
| *Paulo:* | *No problem. Do you have sun block?* |
| Paulo: | Não tem problema. Você tem protetor solar? |
| *Sandra:* | *Yes, I do. Here it is.* |
| Sandra: | Sim, tenho. Aqui está. |
| *Paulo:* | *Thank you!* |
| Paulo: | Obrigado! |

# Take It Further

▶ 3H Take It Further (CD: 1, Track: 27)

You saw how the verb **ter** (*to have*) was conjugated in the affirmative. To form the negative, place **não** (*no*) before the verb:

| | |
|---|---|
| *I don't have* | eu não tenho |
| *he/she doesn't have* | ele/ela não tem |

To form questions, simply put a question mark at the end:

| | |
|---|---|
| *Do you have … ?* | Você tem … ? |
| *Do they have … ?* | Eles/Elas têm … ? |

# ✎ Work Out 2

Complete with the verb **ter,** and then translate.

1. Eu não _____ dinheiro. Você _____ ?

2. Roberto _____ dor de dente.

3. Márcia e Luísa não _____ cachorros. Elas _____ gatos.

4. O professor e os estudantes _____ livros e canetas.

5. O recepcionista _____ uns jornais.

6. Felipe não _____ as chaves.

7. Vocês _____ tempo?

8. Eu e Ana _____ umas fotografias.

**ANSWER KEY**
1. tenho/tem (*I don't have money. Do you?*) 2. tem (*Roberto has a toothache.*) 3. têm/têm (*Márcia and Luisa don't have dogs. They have cats.*) 4. têm (*The teacher and the students have books and pens.*) 5.

tem (*The receptionist has some newspapers.*) 6. tem (*Felipe doesn't have the keys.*) têm (*Do you have time?*) 8. temos (*Ana and I have some photographs.*)

# ✎ Drive It Home

Rewrite the sentences in the plural. Put the subject in the plural too.

**Ex:** A estudante tem um livro. As estudantes têm uns livros.

1. O professor tem um livro.

   _____

2. A amiga tem uma raquete.

   _____

3. O jornal tem uma fotografia.

   _____

4. O hotel tem um quarto.

   _____

5. O homem tem um escritório.

   _____

6. A esposa tem um anel.

   _____

7. O banco tem um cliente.

   _____

8. O gerente tem um problema.

   _____

**ANSWER KEY**

1. Os professores têm uns livros. 2. As amigas têm umas raquetes. 3. Os jornais têm umas fotografias. 4. Os hotéis têm uns quartos. 5. Os homens têm uns escritórios. 6. As esposas têm uns anéis. 7. Os bancos têm uns clientes. 8. Os gerentes têm uns problemas.

## Parting Words

Ótimo! *Great!* You've finished the lesson! By now, you should be able to:

☐ count (Still unsure? Go back to page 44.)

☐ use *a/an* and *some* (Still unsure? Go back to page 46.)

☐ form plurals in Portuguese (Still unsure? Go back to page 46.)

☐ use the verb ter (*to have*) (Still unsure? Go back to page 52.)

☐ put it all together in a short conversation (Still unsure? Go back to page 54.)

Don't forget to practice and reinforce what you've learned by visiting www.livinglanguage.com/languagelab for flashcards, games, and quizzes!

## Take it Further

▶ 3I Take It Further (CD: 1, Track: 28)

### NUMBERS 21-100

| twenty-one | vinte e um/uma |
| twenty-two | vinte e dois/duas |
| twenty-three | vinte e três |
| thirty | trinta |
| thirty-one | trinta e um/uma |

| thirty-two | trinta e dois/duas |
| thirty-three | trinta e três |
| forty | quarenta |
| fifty | cinquenta |
| sixty | sessenta |
| seventy | setenta |
| eighty | oitenta |
| ninety | noventa |
| one hundred | cem |
| one hundred and one | cento e um/uma |
| one hundred and two | cento e dois/duas |
| one hundred and three | cento e três |

You learned that **um** (*one*) and **dois** (*two*) have both masculine and feminine forms. The same is true for higher numbers with **um** or **dois**.

**Há vinte e duas portas.**
*There are twenty-two doors.*

**A casa tem quarenta e duas janelas.**
*The house has forty-two windows.*

# Word Recall

1. How do you ask someone if he has a newspaper?

   Você tem _____ ?

2. How do you ask a receptionist at a hotel if they have a room?

   O hotel tem _____ ?

3. How do you ask a friend if he has a problem?

   Você tem _____ ?

4. How do you tell someone you don't have an aspirin.

   Eu _____ aspirina.

5. How do you tell someone you and your family don't have the keys.

   Nós _____ chaves.

6. How do you tell someone the children don't have a dog.

   As crianças _____ cão.

**ANSWER KEY**
1. um jornal; 2. um quarto; 3. um problema; 4. não tenho uma; 5. não temos as; 6. não têm um

# Lesson 4: Around the House

**Lição Quatro: Em Casa**

**Oi!** *Hi!* In this lesson, you'll learn how to:

☐ use the verb estar (*to be*)

☐ use idiomatic expressions with estar (*to be*)

☐ use the preposition em (*at, on, in*)

☐ use possessive adjectives like *my, your,* and *our*

☐ use what you've learned to talk about things around your home.

**Que legal!** (*Cool!*)

# Vocabulary Builder 1

▷ 4A Vocabulary Builder 1 (CD: 1, Track: 29)

| | |
|---|---|
| *The car is in the garage.* | O carro está na garagem. |
| *The documents are in the drawer.* | Os documentos estão na gaveta. |
| *The towels are in the bathroom.* | As toalhas estão no banheiro. |
| *The shoes are in the closet.* | Os sapatos estão no armário. |
| *The cat is on the armchair.* | O gato está na poltrona. |
| *The books are in the bookcases.* | Os livros estão nas estantes. |
| *The vase is on the table.* | O vaso está na mesa. |
| *There's a swimming pool in the backyard.* | Há uma piscina no quintal. |
| *There are two beds in the bedroom.* | Há duas camas no quarto. |
| *There are three windows in the living room.* | Há três janelas na sala de estar. |
| *There's a refrigerator in the kitchen.* | Há uma geladeira na cozinha. |
| *There's water in the bottle.* | Há água na garrafa. |

# Take It Further

▷ 4B Take It Further (CD: 1, Track: 30)

## PRONOUNCING CONSONANTS

| | | |
|---|---|---|
| r | at the beginning of a word, like a breathy *h* (trilled in some parts of Brazil) | reservar *(to reserve)*, rua *(street)* |

| r | in the middle of a word between vowels, like a tap or a flap against the ridge behind the top teeth | para (*to*), caro (*expensive*) |
|---|---|---|
| r | at the end of a syllable (before another consonant), like a breathy *h*, or a flap in some parts of Brazil | porta (*door*), carne (*meat*) |
| r | at the end of a word, like a breathy *h*, or a flap in some parts of Brazil | senhor (*sir*), bar (*bar*) |
| rr | like a breathy *h* (trilled in some parts of Brazil) | carro (*car*), arroz (*rice*) |
| t | before a, o, u and other consonants like the *t* in *take* | tarde (*afternoon*), todo (*all*) |
| t | before e and i, like the *ch* in *choose* | tia (*aunt*), importante (*important*) |

When you say the word quarto, remember that the r is pronounced like a breathy h, or a flap.

However, just like in the U.S., regional accents can change a bit depending on how people pronounce certain words. People who live in Rio, the cariocas, famously pronounce the r more trilled than paulistanos, who live in São Paulo and soften their r. In small towns, the r can be longer, sounding like the American r.

Keep in mind that most of the time regional differences in how words are pronounced contribute to the charm of a country. In addition, these differences are rarely so strong that they confuse people. Also most media personalities, such as newscasters and radio announcers, speak in what is called standard Brazilian Portuguese, just like it happens in the U.S.

# ✎ Vocabulary Practice 1

Using Vocabulary Builder 1 as a guide, complete the following sentences.

1. **O gato está** _____.

   *The cat is on the armchair.*

2. **Há duas camas** _____.

   *There are two beds in the bedroom.*

3. **Os documentos estão** _____.

   *The documents are in the drawer.*

4. **O carro está** _____.

   *The car is in the garage.*

5. **Os livros estão** _____.

   *The books are in the bookcases.*

6. **Há três janelas** _____.

   *There are three windows in the living room.*

7. **Há uma piscina** _____.

   *There's a swimming pool in the backyard.*

8. **Os sapatos estão** _____.

*The shoes are in the closet.*

9. **As toalhas estão** _____.

*The towels are in the bathroom.*

10. **O vaso está** _____.

*The vase is on the table.*

**ANSWER KEY**
1. na poltrona; 2. no quarto; 3. na gaveta; 4. na garagem; 5. nas estantes; 6. na sala de estar; 7. no quintal; 8. no armário; 9. no banheiro; 10. na mesa

# Grammar Builder 1
▶ 4C Grammar Builder 1 (CD: 1, Track: 31)

## THE VERB ESTAR (*TO BE*)

The verb estar is one of two verbs that mean *to be*. Estar is used to express locations and temporary states and feelings. First let's look at its forms.

| I am | eu estou |
|---|---|
| you are | você está |
| he/she is | ele/ela está |
| we are | nós estamos |
| you are | vocês estão |
| they are | eles/elas estão |

Now, let's study some examples of how to use it.

For locations:

**As crianças estão no parque.**
*The children are in the park.*

As chaves estão na gaveta.
*The keys are in the drawer.*

Eu estou no Brasil.
*I'm in Brazil.*

For temporary states:

Ela está com sede.
*She's thirsty.*

A casa está limpa.
*The house is clean.*

For feelings:

Ela está feliz.
*She's happy.*

Eu estou triste.
*I'm sad.*

To use the verb estar (*to be*) in the negative, put não (*no/not*) before the verb:

Marina e Paulo não estão em casa.
*Marina and Paulo are not home.*

For the interrogative, simply add a question mark to written sentences or use question intonation when speaking.

Pedro está no jardim?
*Is Pedro in the garden?*

## Take It Further

▶ 4D Take It Further (CD: 1, Track: 32)

### THE PREPOSITION EM

In this lesson, you probably noticed the preposition em, which means *at*, *on*, or *in*.
It is usually contracted with the definite article:

| singular | plural |
|---|---|
| em + o = no | em + os = nos |
| em + a = na | em + as = nas |

Há flores no jardim.
*There are flowers in the garden.*

Ele está na estação.
*He is at the station.*

It can also be used alone with other prepositions of place.

| on top of/above | em cima |
|---|---|
| under | embaixo |
| in front of | em frente |

Há um terraço em cima e um embaixo.
*There's a terrace above and one below.*

Há árvores em frente.
*There are trees in front.*

## Vocabulary Builder 2

▶ 4E Vocabulary Builder 2 (CD: 1, Track: 33)

| | |
|---|---|
| *My bicycle is on the sidewalk.* | A minha bicicleta está na calçada. |
| *My handkerchief is in my handbag.* | O meu lenço está na minha bolsa. |
| *Is your wallet in your pocket?* | A sua carteira está no seu bolso? |
| *Your computer is on your desk.* | O seu computador está na sua escrivaninha. |
| *Do you have my address?* | Você tem o meu endereço? |
| *Our mother is at work.* | A nossa mãe está no trabalho. |
| *Our children are on our farm.* | Os nossos filhos estão na nossa fazenda. |
| *Your CDs are on the shelves.* | Os seus CDs estão nas prateleiras. |
| *Your friends (f.) aren't at the birthday party.* | As suas amigas não estão na festa de aniversário. |
| *Your papers are in order.* | Os seus papéis estão em ordem. |

## ✎ Vocabulary Practice 2

Complete the sentences with one of the words in the list below. Use the translation to help you.

endereço, fazenda, bicicleta, carteira, trabalho, lenço, prateleiras, festa de aniversário, papéis, escrivaninha

1. O meu _____ está na minha bolsa.

   *My handkerchief is in my handbag.*

2. As suas amigas não estão na _____?

   *Aren't your friends at the birthday party?*

3. **Os nossos filhos estão na nossa** _____.

   *Our children are on our farm.*

4. **A sua** _____ **está no seu bolso?**

   *Is your wallet in your pocket?*

5. **A minha** _____ **está na calçada.**

   *My bicycle is on the sidewalk.*

6. **Os seus CDs estão nas** _____.

   *Your CDs are on the shelves.*

7. **A nossa mãe está no** _____.

   *Our mother is at work.*

8. **Os seus** _____ **estão em ordem.**

   *Your papers are in order.*

9. **O seu computador está na sua** _____.

   *Your computer is on your desk.*

10. **Você tem o meu** _____?

    *Do you have my address?*

    **ANSWER KEY**
    1. lenço; 2. festa de aniversário; 3. fazenda; 4. carteira; 5. bicicleta; 6. prateleiras; 7. trabalho; 8. papéis; 9. escrivaninha; 10. endereço

# Grammar Builder 2

▶ 4F Grammar Builder 2 (CD: 1, Track: 34)

## POSSESSIVE ADJECTIVES

You may have noticed that the sentences in Vocabulary Builder 2 contained some possessive adjectives.

A possessive adjective is a kind of adjective that shows possession, like the English *my*, *your*, *his*, *her*, *our*, and *their*. In Portuguese, possessive adjectives have masculine, feminine, singular and plural forms.

Some possessive adjectives agree in gender and number with the thing possessed:

| SINGULAR | PLURAL |
| --- | --- |
| o meu carro | os meus carros |
| *my car* | *my cars* |
| a minha casa | as minhas casas |
| *my house* | *my houses* |
| o seu carro | os seus carros |
| *your car* | *your cars* |
| a sua casa | as suas casas |
| *your house* | *your houses* |
| o nosso carro | os nossos carros |
| *our car* | *our cars* |
| a nossa casa | as nossas casas |
| *our house* | *our houses* |

But the equivalents of *his*, *her*, and *their* do not.

| o carro dele | o carro dela |
| --- | --- |
| *his car* | *her car* |

| a casa dele *his house* | a casa dela *her house* |
|---|---|
| o carro deles *their car*—for masculine or mixed group  os carros deles *their cars*—for masculine or mixed group | o carro delas *their car*—for feminine  os carros delas *their cars*—for feminine |
| a casa deles *their house*—for masculine or mixed group  as casas deles *their houses*—for masculine or mixed group | a casa delas *their house*—for feminine  as casas delas *their houses*—for feminine |

Let's see how they're used in sentences.

Ele está no apartamento dele e ela está no apartamento dela.
*He is in his apartment and she is in her apartment.*

As meninas têm o gato delas e os meninos têm o gato deles também.
*The girls have their cat and the boys have their cat too.*

As meninas têm os livros delas e os meninos têm os livros deles.
*The girls have their books and the boys have their books.*

# ✎ Work Out 1

A. Complete the sentences below with a possessive adjective from the list below.

meu, nosso, minha, nossos, suas

1. A _____ bicicleta está na garagem.

   *My bicycle is in the garage.*

2. Os _____ documentos não estão na gaveta.

   *Our documents are not in the drawer.*

3. O _____ gato está no jardim?

   *Is our cat in the garden?*

4. As _____ toalhas estão no banheiro.

   *Your towels are in the bathroom.*

5. O _____ pai está na fazenda.

   *Our father is on the farm.*

B. Now, complete these sentences with a possessive adjective from the list below.
   deles (2), delas, dele (2), dela

1. Paulo tem as chaves _____.

   *Paulo has his keys.*

2. Mariana não está no escritório _____.

   *Mariana isn't in her office.*

3. Sérgio e Tomás estão nas casas _____.

   *Sergio and Tomas are at their houses.*

4. As crianças têm os quartos _____.

   *The children have their bedrooms.*

5. O professor tem o livro _____ e os estudantes têm os livros

_____.

*The teacher has his book and the students have theirs.*

**ANSWER KEY**
A. 1. minha; 2. nossos; 3. nosso; 4. suas; 5. nosso
B. 1. dele; 2. dela; 3. deles; 4. delas; 5. dele/deles

## Take It Further

4G Take It Further (CD: 1, Track: 35)

### IDIOMATIC EXPRESSIONS WITH ESTAR COM (*TO BE WITH*)

Estar com (*to be with*) is used to express a momentary or passing feeling or state.

| to be thirsty | estar com sede |
|---|---|
| to be hungry | estar com fome |
| to be cold | estar com frio |
| to be sleepy | estar com sono |
| to be hot | estar com calor |
| to be in a hurry | estar com pressa |
| to be afraid | estar com medo |
| to be embarrassed | estar com vergonha |
| to have a headache | estar com dor de cabeça |
| to have a fever | estar com febre |

Here are some more common expressions with the verb estar (*to be*).

| it's raining | está chovendo |
|---|---|
| it's windy | está ventando |
| it's snowing | está nevando |

| it's sunny | está ensolarado |
|---|---|
| it's overcast | está nublado |

## 🔊 Bring It All Together

▶ 4H Bring It All Together (CD: 1, Track: 36)

| | |
|---|---|
| *Son:* | *Mom, are my magazines there?* |
| **Filho:** | **Mãe, as minhas revistas estão aí?** |
| *Mother:* | *No, they aren't here. Your magazines are on your desk in your bedroom.* |
| **Mãe:** | **Não, elas não estão aqui. As suas revistas estão na sua escrivaninha no seu quarto.** |
| *Daughter:* | *Mom, are my shoes down there?* |
| **Filha:** | **Mãe, os meus sapatos estão aí embaixo?** |
| *Mother:* | *No, Mariana. Your shoes are up there in your closet.* |
| **Mãe:** | **Não, Mariana, os seus sapatos estão aí em cima no seu armário.** |
| *Father:* | *Dear, is the cat there in the living room?* |
| **Pai:** | **Querida, o gato está aí na sala de estar?** |
| *Mother:* | *No, the cat is under the table in the garden, dear.* |
| **Mãe:** | **Não, o gato está embaixo da mesa no jardim, querido.** |
| *Daughter:* | *Mom, is grandma home?* |
| **Filha:** | **Mãe, a vovó está em casa?** |
| *Mother:* | *Yes, but she's in her bedroom. She's sleepy.* |
| **Mãe:** | **Sim, mas ela está no quarto dela. Ela está com sono.** |
| *Son:* | *Mom, I'm thirsty.* |
| **Filho:** | **Mãe, estou com sede.** |
| *Mother:* | *There's water in the bottle in the kitchen.* |
| **Mãe:** | **Há água na garrafa na cozinha.** |
| *Mother:* | *I think I have a headache!* |
| **Mãe:** | **Acho que eu estou com dor de cabeça!** |

## ✎ Work Out 2

Complete the following sentences with the verb estar (*to be*).

1. Os estudantes _____ na escola.

   *The students are in school.*

2. As chaves _____ na gaveta.

   *The keys are in the drawer.*

3. Eu não _____ com medo.

   *I'm not afraid.*

4. O meu primo _____ na casa dele.

   *My cousin is at his home.*

5. Você e as suas amigas _____ na festa de aniversário?

   *Are you and your friends at the birthday party?*

6. A garrafa _____ na geladeira?

   *Is the bottle in the refrigerator?*

7. O livro e a revista _____ na estante.

   *The book and the magazine are in the bookcase.*

8. O meu amigo não _____ na casa dele.

   *My friend is not in his house.*

9. Maria, você _____ com fome?

   *Maria, are you hungry?*

10. **Eu e minha irmã** _____ **com frio.**

*My sister and I are cold.*

**ANSWER KEY**
1. estão; 2. estão; 3. estou; 4. está; 5. estão; 6. está; 7. estão; 8. está; 9. está; 10. estamos

# ✎ Drive It Home

Write sentences using the cues in parentheses. Follow the example.

Ex. **Você/apartamento** (*You're in your apartment.*)
**Você está no seu apartamento.**

1. **Nós/escola** (*We're in our school.*)

   _____

2. **Vocês/escritórios** (*You're in your offices.*)

   _____

3. **Eu/poltrona** (*I'm in my armchair.*)

   _____

4. **Você/quarto** (*You're in your bedroom.*)

   _____

5. **Nós/jardim** (*We're in our garden.*)

   _____

6. **Ele/carro** (*He's in his car.*)

   _____

7. **Ela/casa** (*She's in her house.*)

   _____

8. **Eles/apartamentos** (*They're in their apartments.*)

---

**ANSWER KEY**

1. **Nós estamos na nossa escola. 2. Vocês estão nos seus escritórios. 3. Eu estou na minha poltrona. 4. Você está no seu quarto. 5. Nós estamos no nosso jardim. 6. Ele está no carro dele. 7. Ela está na casa dela. 8. Eles estão nos apartamentos deles.**

## Parting Words

**Muito bem!** *Very good!* You've finished the lesson! How did you do? You should be able to:

☐ use the verb **estar** (*to be*) (Still unsure? Go back to page 61.)

☐ use idiomatic expressions with **estar** (*to be*) (Still unsure? Go back to page 64.)

☐ use the preposition **em** (*at, on, in*) (Still unsure? Go back to page 66.)

☐ use possessive adjectives like *my*, *your*, and *our* (Still unsure? Go back to page 69.)

☐ use what you've learned to talk about things around your home (Still unsure? Go back to page 73.)

Don't forget to practice and reinforce what you've learned by visiting www.livinglanguage.com/languagelab for flashcards, games, and quizzes!

# Word Recall

Fill in the floor plan below based on the vocabulary you've learned.

Floor Plan

1. _____
2. _____
3. _____
4. _____

**ANSWER KEY**
1. o quarto; 2. o banheiro; 3. a sala de estar; 4. a cozinha

# Lesson 5: Describing People and Things

## Lição Cinco: Descrevendo Pessoas e Coisas

In this lesson, you'll learn how to:

☐ use colors and other common adjectives in Portuguese

☐ describe people and things

☐ use the verb ser (*to be*)

☐ use possessive words like *mine, yours,* and *ours*

☐ put it all together in a brief conversation

**Fantástico!** *Fantastic!*

# Vocabulary Builder 1

5A Vocabulary Builder 1 (CD 1, Track 37)

| | |
|---|---|
| *The tomato is red.* | O tomate é vermelho. |
| *The bananas are yellow.* | As bananas são amarelas. |
| *The sky is blue.* | O céu é azul. |
| *The sea is green.* | O mar é verde. |
| *The bird is pink.* | O pássaro é cor-de-rosa. |
| *The chair is orange.* | A cadeira é laranja. |
| *The movie is black and white.* | O filme é preto e branco. |
| *The horse is brown.* | O cavalo é marrom. |
| *The gate is gray.* | O portão é cinza. |
| *The t-shirts are purple.* | As camisetas são roxas. |

# Vocabulary Practice 1

Match the Portuguese on the left with the English equivalent on the right.

1. branco        a. *purple*

2. preto        b. *red*

3. azul        c. *green*

4. vermelho        d. *yellow*

5. verde        e. *blue*

6. amarelo        f. *white*

7. roxo        g. *orange*

8. cor-de-rosa        h. *black*

9. laranja        i. *brown*

10. marrom        j. *gray*

11. cinza        k. *pink*

# Grammar Builder 1

▶ 5B Grammar Builder 1 (CD 1, Track 38)

## ADJECTIVES

Unlike English, in which the adjective comes before the noun it modifies, in Portuguese adjectives usually follow the noun. Look at the example below.

a praia bonita
*the beautiful beach*

When you use an adjective to describe a noun in Portuguese, it needs to agree with the noun in gender and number.

Some adjectives are regular and have the familiar endings o (m./sg.), os (m./pl.) or a (f./sg.) and as (f./pl.):

|           | SINGULAR                           | PLURAL                               |
|-----------|------------------------------------|--------------------------------------|
| masculine | o carro pequeno                    | os carros pequenos                   |
|           | *the small car*                    | *the small cars*                     |
| feminine  | a casa pequena                     | as casas pequenas                    |
|           | *the small house*                  | *the small houses*                   |

The same is true for colors. The adjectives *white* (branco), *black* (preto), *yellow* (amarelo), and *red* (vermelho) agree in number and gender with the noun like the examples above:

um carro preto
*a black car*

duas camisetas pretas
*two black t-shirts*

Adjectives that end in e or in a consonant usually have just one form for the singular, and one form for the plural.

| | |
|---|---|
| o quarto grande | os quartos grandes |
| *the big room* | *the big rooms* |
| a mesa grande | as mesas grandes |
| *the big table* | *the big tables* |
| o homem jovem | os homens jovens |
| *the young man* | *the young men* |
| a mulher jovem | as mulheres jovens |
| *the young woman* | *the young women* |
| o mar azul | os mares azuis |
| *the blue sea* | *the blue seas* |
| a caneta azul | as canetas azuis |
| *the blue pen* | *the blue pens* |

There are a few irregular adjectives, for example bom (*good*) and mau (*bad*). Here, the adjective comes before the noun.

| | |
|---|---|
| o bom livro | os bons livros |
| *the good book* | *the good books* |
| a boa revista | as boas revistas |
| *the good magazine* | *the good magazines* |
| o mau aluno | os maus alunos |
| *the bad student* | *the bad students* |
| a má aluna | as más alunas |
| *the bad student* | *the bad students* |

The colors *pink* (cor-de-rosa), *orange* (laranja), and *gray* (cinza) do not vary:

a xícara cor-de-rosa
*the pink cup*

os sofás cor-de-rosa
*the pink sofas*

## Vocabulary Builder 2

▷ 5C Vocabulary Builder 2 (CD 2, Track 1)

| *He is thin.* | Ele é magro. |
| *She is short.* | Ela é baixa. |
| *We are strong.* | Nós somos fortes. |
| *They are good.* | Elas são boas. |
| *You are young.* | Você é jovem. |
| *The coat is new.* | O casaco é novo. |
| *The city is modern.* | A cidade é moderna. |
| *My glasses are old.* | Os meus óculos são velhos. |
| *The mountains are big.* | As montanhas são grandes. |
| *The countries are small.* | Os países são pequenos. |
| *The buildings are tall/high.* | Os prédios são altos. |

## ✎ Vocabulary Practice 2

Complete the sentences with the correct adjective. Make sure it agrees with the
noun in gender and number!

1. Você é _____.

   *You are young.*

2. **A cidade é** _____.

   *The city is new.*

3. **Ela é** _____.

   *She is short.*

4. **Ele é** _____.

   *He is thin.*

5. **Nós somos** _____.

   *We are strong.*

6. **As montanhas são** _____.

   *The mountains are big.*

7. **Elas são** _____.

   *They are good.*

8. **Os prédios são** _____.

   *The buildings are tall.*

9. **Paulo e eu somos** _____.

   *Paulo and I are Brazilian.*

10. **Os óculos são** _____.

    *The glasses are old.*

11. **Os países são** _____.

    *The countries are small.*

12. **O casaco é** _____.

    *The coat is new.*

**ANSWER KEY**

1. jovem; 2. nova; 3. baixa; 4. magro; 5. fortes; 6. grandes; 7. boas; 8. altos; 9. brasileiros; 10. velhos; 11. pequenos; 12. novo

# Grammar Builder 2

⊳ 5D Grammar Builder 2 (CD 2, Track 2)

## THE VERB SER (*TO BE*)

First, let's look at the forms of this irregular verb:

| | |
|---|---|
| *I am* | eu sou |
| *you are* | você é |
| *he is* | ele é |
| *she is* | ela é |
| *we are* | nós somos |
| *you are* | vocês são |
| *they are* | eles/elas são |

In Lesson 4 you learned the verb estar (*to be*), which is used for locations, and temporary states and feelings. Ser also means *to be*, but it is used differently.

Ser is used to describe inherent characteristics of people, places and things. It is also used with professions and nationalities.

Ela é alta.
*She is tall.*

Tomates são vermelhos.
*Tomatoes are red.*

Eu sou arquiteto.
*I am an architect.*

**Ele é japonês.**
*He is Japanese.*

## Take It Further

▶ 5E Take It Further (CD 2, Track 3)

### PREPOSITION DE (*OF*)

A very common and useful preposition in Portuguese is de, which means *of* or *from*, as in:

**Eu sou de Nova Iorque.**
*I'm from New York.*

When de comes right before a definite article, meaning *of the*, it forms a contraction:

de + o = do
de + os = dos
de + a = da
de + as = das

De is used to express possession:

**O carro é do Paulo.**
*The car is Paulo's.*

**Ele está na casa da Maria.**
*He's at Maria's house.*

De is also used to indicate origin or nationality.

**Mário é da Itália e Ana é do Brasil.**
*Mario is from Italy and Ana is from Brazil.*

---

# ✎ Work Out 1

A. Rewrite the following sentences in the plural.

1. **Ele é alto.**

   *He is tall.*

   _____

2. **Ela é magra.**

   *She is thin.*

   _____

3. **Você é americano?**

   *Are you American?*

   _____

4. **Eu não sou australiana.**

   *I'm not Australian.*

   _____

5. **O filme não é bom.**

   *The movie isn't good.*

   _____

B. Now, put the following sentences in the singular.

1. **Nós somos professores.**

   *We are teachers.*

2. **As cidades são modernas.**

   *The cities are modern.*

3. **As praias são bonitas.**

   *The beaches are beautiful.*

4. **Os turistas não são alemães.**

   *The tourists are not German.*

5. **As poltronas são confortáveis?**

   *Are the armchairs comfortable?*

**ANSWER KEY**
A. 1. Eles são altos. 2. Elas são magras. 3.Vocês são americanos? 4. Nós não somos australianas. 5. Os filmes não são bons.
B. 1. Eu sou professor. 2. A cidade é moderna. 3. A praia é bonita. 4. O turista não é alemão. 5. A poltrona é confortável?

# Bring It All Together

▶ 5F Bring It All Together (CD 2, Track 4)

| Mary: | *Rafael, are you from Brazil?* |
| Mary: | Rafael, você é do Brasil? |

| Rafael: | Yes, I am but my mother's not Brazilian. She's from Argentina. She's from Buenos Aires. |
| --- | --- |
| Rafael: | **Sou sim, mas minha mãe não é brasileira. Ela é da Argentina. Ela é de Buenos Aires.** |
| Mary: | You're from which city? |
| Mary: | **Você é de que cidade?** |
| Rafael: | I'm from Florianopolis, in the south of Brazil. |
| Rafael: | **Sou de Florianópolis, no sul do Brasil.** |
| Mary: | Are the beaches there beautiful? |
| Mary: | **As praias lá são bonitas?** |
| Rafael: | Yes, they're very beautiful. The sea is blue and the mountains are very green. |
| Rafael: | **São muito bonitas. O mar é azul e as montanhas são muito verdes.** |
| Mary: | Is Florianopolis a big or a small city? |
| Mary: | **Florianópolis é uma cidade grande ou pequena?** |
| Rafael: | It's a medium-size city. It's not big like São Paulo. And you, Mary? What city are you from? |
| Rafael: | **É uma cidade média. Não é grande como São Paulo. E você, Mary? De que cidade você é?** |
| Mary: | I'm from Denver. Denver is a big city in the West of the United States. There isn't a sea, but the mountains are very big and very high. |
| Mary: | **Eu sou de Denver. Denver é uma cidade grande no oeste dos Estados Unidos. Não há mar em Denver, mas há montanhas muito grandes e muito altas.** |

# ✎ Work Out 2

Complete the sentences with an adjective according to the translation. Don't forget to make the adjective agree in gender and number with the noun!

1. **O pássaro é** _____ .

   *The bird is yellow.*

2. **As flores são** _____ .

   *The flowers are white.*

3. **Os turistas são** _____ .

   *The tourists are American.*

4. **A minha amiga é** _____ .

   *My friend is beautiful.*

5. **Ele tem uma casa muito** _____ ?

   *Does he have a very small house?*

6. **As garrafas não são** _____ .

   *The bottles aren't big.*

7. **O computador dele não é** _____ .

   *His computer isn't old.*

8. **As revistas** _____ **estão em cima da mesa.**

   *The new magazines are on the table.*

9. **Há** _____ **professores e há professores ruins.**

   *There are good teachers and there are bad teachers.*

10. **As maçãs argentinas são muito _____.**

*Argentine apples are very good.*

**ANSWER KEY**

1. amarelo; 2. brancas; 3. americanos; 4. bonita; 5. pequena; 6. grandes; 7. velho; 8. novas; 9. bons; 10. boas

## Take It Further

▶ 5G Take It Further (CD 2, Track 5)

In Lesson 4 you learned the possessive adjectives: meu, minha (*my*), seu, sua (*your*), nosso, nossa (*our*), dele (*his*), dela (*her*), along with their plurals. They're called possessive adjectives because they take the place of an adjective, as in this example: meu livro (*my book*).

There are also possessive pronouns which take the place of a noun. In English these are *mine, yours, his, hers, ours, theirs*. So you say: *this is my book* or *this book is mine*. In Portuguese the possessive pronouns are the same as the possessive adjectives.

O meu carro é azul.
*My car is blue.*

O carro azul é meu.
*The blue car is mine.*

A nossa casa é amarela.
*Our house is yellow.*

A casa amarela é nossa.
*The yellow house is ours.*

# ✎ Drive It Home

Complete the sentences with the correct forms of ser or estar. Remember that ser is used to express inherent or permanent qualities, nationalities and occupations, and fixed or geographical locations. Estar is used to express temporary locations, states and feelings.

1. O meu casaco _____ vermelho.

   *My coat is red.*

2. Eu _____ arquiteto e eu _____ no escritório.

   *I am an architect and I'm at the office.*

3. As montanhas _____ muito grandes.

   *The mountains are very big.*

4. Meus primos _____ brasileiros.

   *My cousins are Brazilian.*

5. Vocês não _____ com fome, mas _____ com sede.

   *You aren't hungry but you're thirsty.*

6. A minha bolsa _____ preta e ela _____ no armário.

   *My handbag is black and it's in the closet.*

7. O carro azul _____ nosso e ele _____ na rua.

   *Our car is blue and it's on the street.*

8. Paulo e eu _____ de férias. Nós _____ na Itália.

   *Paulo and I are on vacation. We're in Italy.*

9. A cama do hotel _____ grande, mas não _____ confortável.

   *The bed in the hotel is big, but it's not comfortable.*

10. **Nós** _____ **estudantes e nós** _____ **na escola.**

*We're students and we're at school.*

**ANSWER KEY**
1. é; 2. sou, estou; 3. são; 4. são; 5. estão, estão; 6. é, está; 7. é, está; 8. estamos, estamos; 9. é, é; 10. somos, estamos

# Parting Words

**Excelente!** *Excellent!* You've finished the lesson! How did you do? By now, you should be able to:

☐ use colors and other common adjectives in Portuguese (Still unsure? Go back to page 79.)

☐ describe people and things (Still unsure? Go back to page 80.)

☐ use the verb ser (*to be*) (Still unsure? Go back to page 84.)

☐ put it together in a brief conversation (Still unsure? Go back to page 87.)

☐ use possessive words like *mine, yours,* and *ours* (Still unsure? Go back to page 90.)

Don't forget to practice and reinforce what you've learned by visiting www.livinglanguage.com/languagelab for flashcards, games, and quizzes!

# Word Recall

Describe a garden by answering the following questions.

1. How do you say *garden, flowers* and *cat* in Portuguese?

   _____

2. How do you say, *it's a beautiful garden?*

   O _____ é _____ .

3. How do you say, *there are some yellow and some white flowers in the garden?*

   Há umas _____ e _____

   no _____ .

4. How do you say, *there's a cat in the garden?*

   _____ um _____ no _____ .

5. How do you say, *the cat is black and white?*

   O _____ é _____ e _____ .

6. How do you say, *there's a chair in the garden?*

   _____ uma _____ no _____ .

7. How do you say, *the chair is red?*

   A _____ .

8. How do you say, *the cat is on the red chair?*

   O _____ na _____ .

**ANSWER KEY**

1. jardim/flores/gato; 2. O jardim é bonito. 3. Há umas flores amarelas e brancas no jardim. 4. Há um gato no jardim. 5. O gato é preto e branco. 6. Há uma cadeira no jardim. 7. A cadeira é vermelha. 8. O gato está na cadeira vermelha.

# Quiz 1

Let's see how you're doing. Here's a short quiz testing the material in Lessons 1-5. Answer all the questions, and then score yourself to see if you could use a refresher. If you find that you need to go back and review, please do so before continuing on to Lesson Six.

Ready?

A. Match the Portuguese expression with the English translation.

1. obrigado          a. *how are you?*
2. bom dia         b. *please*
3. bem-vindo       c. *thank you*
4. como vai você?    d. *welcome*
5. por favor        e. *good morning*

B. Match the numbers.

1. 95         a. trinta e sete
2. 102        b. noventa e cinco
3. 37         c. vinte e oito
4. 84         d. oitenta e quatro
5. 28         e. cento e dois

C. Match the sentences in Portuguese with the English translation.

1. Nós temos uma garagem em casa.    a. *The cars are ours.*

2. A garagem de casa é grande.

3. Há três carros na garagem.

4. Os carros estão na garagem.

5. Os carros são nossos.

b. *There are three cars in the garage.*

c. *The cars are in the garage.*

d. *The garage at home is big.*

e. *We have a garage at home.*

D. Complete the sentences with the correct pair of possessive adjectives from the list below then translate the sentences.

sua/dela, suas/seu, meu/nosso, minhas/seu, nossos/deles

1. Os _____ primos estão na casa _____ .

2. As _____ amigas estão no _____ apartamento?

3. A _____ carteira está na bolsa _____ ?

4. O _____ casaco está no _____ carro.

5. As _____ chaves estão no _____ bolso?

**ANSWER KEY**
A. 1. c; 2. e; 3. d; 4. a; 5. b
B. 1. b; 2. e; 3. a; 4. d; 5. c
C. 1. e; 2. d; 3. b; 4. c; 5. a
D. 1. nossos, deles (*Our cousins are in their house.*) 2. minhas, seu (*Are my friends in your apartment?*)
3. sua, dela (*Is your wallet in her handbag?*) 4. meu, nosso (*My coat is in our car.*) 5. minhas, seu (*Are my keys in your pocket?*)

## How Did You Do?

Give yourself a point for every correct answer, then use the following key to determine whether or not you're ready to move on:

**0–7 points:** It's probably best to go back and study the lessons again to make sure you understood everything completely. Take your time; it's not a race! Make sure you spend time reviewing the vocabulary and reading through each Grammar Builder section carefully.

**8–16 points:** If the questions you missed were in sections A or B, you may want to review the vocabulary from previous lessons again; if you missed answers mostly in sections C or D, check the Grammar Builder sections to make sure you have your grammar basics down.

**17–20 points:** Feel free to move on to Lesson Six! You're doing a great job.

|  |  |
|--|--|
|  |  | points

# Lesson 6: Around Town

**Lição Seis: Na Cidade**

By the end of this lesson, you'll be able to:

☐ use important vocabulary for getting around town

☐ express location and direction

☐ ask questions

☐ use ordinal numbers

☐ ask for and give directions

**Já é a sua sexta lição!** *It's already your sixth lesson!*

## Vocabulary Builder 1

▶ 6A Vocabulary Builder 1 (CD 2, Track 6)

| | |
|---|---|
| *The bar is open.* | O bar está aberto. |
| *The restaurants are closed.* | Os restaurantes estão fechados. |
| *The hospital is near.* | O hospital é perto. |
| *The police station is far.* | A delegacia de polícia é longe. |
| *The emergency room is at the corner.* | O pronto socorro é na esquina. |
| *The library is in the middle of the block.* | A biblioteca é no meio da quadra. |
| *The shopping mall has parking.* | O shopping center tem estacionamento. |
| *Is there a bakery near here?* | Há uma padaria perto daqui? |
| *The post office is next to the bank.* | O correio é ao lado do banco. |
| *There's an ATM opposite the hotel.* | Há um caixa eletrônico em frente ao hotel. |
| *Is there a bus station near here?* | Há uma estação rodoviária perto daqui? |
| *There's a taxi stand on the next block.* | Há um ponto de táxi no próximo quarteirão. |
| *Is there a subway in the city?* | Há um metrô na cidade? |
| *The box office is on the right.* | A bilheteria é à direita. |
| *The art museum is on the left.* | O museu de arte é à esquerda. |

## Take It Further

▶ 6B Take It Further (CD 2, Track 7)

In future lessons you'll study the preposition a, which means *to*. For now, observe how it contracts with the definite article a (*the*) and becomes à (*to the/on the*).

A escada rolante é à direita da porta.
*The escalator is to the right of the door.*

O banco é à esquerda do supermercado.
*The bank is to the left of the supermarket.*

---

# ✎ Vocabulary Practice 1

Match the Portuguese words or phrases on the left to the English translation on the right.

| | |
|---|---|
| 1. à esquerda | a. *at the corner* |
| 2. à direita | b. *opposite* or *in front of* |
| 3. na esquina | c. *near here* |
| 4. no meio da quadra | d. *on the left* |
| 5. em frente | e. *open* |
| 6. perto daqui | f. *on the next block* |
| 7. longe | g. *on the right* |
| 8. aberto | h. *closed* |
| 9. fechado | i. *far* |
| 10. no próximo quarteirão | j. *in the middle of the block* |

**ANSWER KEY**
1. d; 2.g; 3. a; 4. j; 5. b; 6. c; 7. i; 8. e; 9. h; 10. f

# Grammar Builder 1

▶ 6C Grammar Builder 1 (CD 2, Track 8)

## THE QUESTION WORDS ONDE (*WHERE*) AND QUEM (*WHO*)

You already know how to ask simple *yes-no* questions in Portuguese, so now let's look at questions with the question words onde (*where*) and quem (*who*).

Unlike English, you don't need inversions or auxiliaries to ask questions using question words in Portuguese. Just begin your sentence with the question word.

**Onde é o correio?**
*Where is the post office?*

**Quem é a pessoa à esquerda?**
*Who is the person on the left?*

## Take It Further

▶ 6D Take It Further (CD 2, Track 9)

### NÚMEROS ORDINAIS (*ORDINAL NUMBERS*)

Ordinal numbers are used to show a sequence or order. Let's look at *first* through *tenth*.

| | |
|---|---|
| *first* | **primeiro** |
| *second* | **segundo** |
| *third* | **terceiro** |
| *fourth* | **quarto** |
| *fifth* | **quinto** |
| *sixth* | **sexto** |
| *seventh* | **sétimo** |
| *eighth* | **oitavo** |
| *ninth* | **nono** |
| *tenth* | **décimo** |

Ordinal numbers are adjectives, so they agree in gender and number with the noun.

**O banco é no segundo quarteirão.**
*The bank is on the second block.*

In Portuguese the ordinal numbers are abbreviated with the superscript ° for masculine and the superscript ª for feminine.

**Ele está no 1º ano.**
*He's in the 1st year.*

**Ele está na 3ª série.**
*He's in 3rd grade.*

## Vocabulary Builder 2

▶ 6E Vocabulary Builder 2 (CD 2, Track 10)

| | |
|---|---|
| *Where's the bathroom?* | Onde é o banheiro? |
| *The bathroom is the first door on the left.* | O banheiro é a primeira porta à esquerda. |
| *Where is the newsstand?* | Onde é a banca de jornais? |
| *The newsstand is in the square.* | A banca de jornais é na praça. |
| *Where's the shoe shop?* | Onde é a loja de sapatos? |
| *It is on the third floor to the right of the elevator.* | É no terceiro andar à direita do elevador. |
| *Where's the airport?* | Onde é o aeroporto? |
| *The airport is 15 kilometers from here.* | O aeroporto é a quinze quilômetros daqui. |

| Where's the embassy? | Onde é a embaixada? |
| The embassy is in the nation's capital. | A embaixada é na capital do país. |
| Where's the service station? | Onde é o posto de gasolina? |
| Turn right at the second traffic light. | Vire à direita no segundo semáforo. |
| Who's the boss? | Quem é o chefe? |
| Who's in the office today? | Quem está no escritório hoje? |
| Who are they? | Quem são eles? |

# ✎ Vocabulary Practice 2

Answer the following questions by unscrambling the words in parentheses.

1. Onde é o banheiro? (*Where's the bathroom?*)

   (banheiro/esquerda/à/primeira/o/é/a/porta)

   _____

2. Onde é o posto de gasolina? (*Where's the service station?*)

   (segundo/à/semáforo/direita/vire /no)

   _____

3. Onde é a banca de jornais? (*Where's the newsstand?*)

   (a/banca/de/praça/é/na/jornais)

   _____

4. Onde é a loja de sapatos? (*Where's the shoe shop?*)

   (do/no/à/andar/elevador/direita/é /terceiro)

   _____

5. **Onde é o aeroporto?** *(Where's the airport?)*

(aeroporto/daqui/é/o/quilômetros/quinze/a)

_____

**ANSWER KEY**

1. O banheiro é a primeira porta à esquerda. 2. Vire à direita no segundo semáforo. 3. A banca de jornais é na praça. 4. É no terceiro andar à direita do elevador. 5. O aeroporto é a quinze quilômetros daqui.

# Take It Further

When writing or saying addresses in Portuguese, you should say the name of the street before the number. Note that when writing you use commas to separate the name of the street, the number, and the floor. Look at the example that includes the zip code (CEP).

| Hotel Plaza | Plaza Hotel |
|---|---|
| Rua da Independência, 39, 4º andar | *39 Rua da Independencia, 4th floor* |
| 01234-000 Salvador, Bahia | *01234-000 Salvador, Bahia* |

Besides **rua** *(street)*, Portuguese also has **avenida** *(avenue)*, **alameda** *(boulevard)*, **estrada** *(road)*, and **rodovia** *(highway)*.

# Grammar Builder 2

▶ 6F Grammar Builder 2 (CD 2, Track 11)

## MORE QUESTION WORDS

**Qual** is used in questions that ask to identify or to choose. Note that in English **qual** can mean either *what* or *which*.

| *What's the way to the airport?* | **Qual é o caminho para o aeroporto?** |
|---|---|
| *What's your address?* | **Qual é o seu endereço?** |

| What's his last name? | Qual é o sobrenome dele? |
| Which is our bus? | Qual é o nosso ônibus? |

**Que** or **o que** (*what*) is used to ask *what thing* or *things*.

| What car do you have? | Que carro você tem? |
| What time is it? | Que horas são? |
| What does he have? | O que ele tem? |
| What's in your bag? | O que há na sua bolsa? |

When asking the frequency with which something happens you use **quando**
which means both *when* and *how often*.

**Quando você escuta música? Eu sempre escuto música à noite.**
*When do you listen to music? I always listen to music at night.*

You can also ask **quantas vezes** (*how many times*) + the expected frequency.

| How many times a day do you brush your teeth? | Quantas vezes por dia você escova os dentes? |
| How many times a week do you study Portuguese? | Quantas vezes por semana você estuda português? |
| How many times a month do pilots travel? | Quantas vezes por mês os pilotos viajam? |

When asking *why* or *how*, use **por que** and **como**:

| Why do you wake up early? Because I work at 7:00 a.m. | Por que você acorda cedo? Porque trabalho às sete horas. |
| How does he wake up early? He uses an alarm clock. | Como ele acorda cedo? Ele usa um despertador. |

Note that to answer a question with the two-word interrogative **por que** (*why*),
you use the one-word conjunction **porque** (*because*).

# ✎ Work Out 1

Complete the sentences with an appropriate Portuguese word. Use the English translation as a guide.

1. Qual o seu _____?

   *What's your address?*

2. Onde é a _____?

   *Where's the newsstand?*

3. Qual o seu _____?

   *What's your last name?*

4. Onde é a _____?

   *Where's the bus station?*

5. _____ são os nossos professores?

   *Who are our teachers?*

6. _____ o caminho para a praia?

   *What's the way to the beach?*

7. _____ você tem na sua bolsa?

   *What's in your bag?*

8. _____ é a biblioteca?

   *Where's the library?*

**ANSWER KEY**
1.endereço; 2. banca de jornais; 3. sobrenome; 4. estação rodoviária; 5. Quem; 6. Qual; 7. O que; 8. Onde

## Bring It All Together

6G Bring It All Together (CD 2, Track 12)

| | |
|---|---|
| Tourist: | Excuse me, ma'am. Where's the post office please? |
| Turista: | Com licença, senhora. Onde é o correio, por favor? |
| Passerby: | The post office is on the second block to the right, but today it is closed. Today is a holiday. |
| Passante: | O correio é na segunda quadra à direita, mas hoje está fechado. Hoje é feriado. |
| Tourist: | And is the bank open? |
| Turista: | E o banco está aberto? |
| Passerby: | No, sir. The bank is also closed. |
| Passante: | Não, senhor. O banco está fechado também. |
| Tourist: | Where is there an ATM? |
| Turista: | Onde há um caixa eletrônico? |
| Passerby: | There's an ATM next to the pharmacy. Turn right on the second street and then make the first left. |
| Passante: | Há um caixa eletrônico ao lado da farmácia. Vire a segunda rua à direita e depois a primeira à esquerda. |
| Tourist: | What holiday is it? |
| Turista: | Que feriado é? |
| Passerby: | Today it is Tiradentes. |
| Passante: | Hoje é Tiradentes. |
| Tourist: | Sorry, one more question. Who is Tiradentes? |
| Turista: | Desculpe, mais uma pergunta. Quem é Tiradentes? |
| Passerby: | Tiradentes is a national hero. |
| Passante: | Tiradentes é um herói nacional. |
| Tourist: | Thank you. |
| Turista: | Muito obrigado. |

# ✎ Work Out 2

A. Translate the following from Portuguese to English.

1. está aberto _____

2. é na esquina _____

3. é na praça _____

4. quem é _____

5. onde é _____

B. Now, Translate from English to Portuguese.

1. *your address* _____

2. *last name* _____

3. *the second traffic light* _____

4. *on the right* _____

5. *near here* _____

C. Complete with the correct ordinal number.

1. É a _____ rua à direita.

   *It's the fourth street on the right.*

2. Vire no _____ semáforo.

   *Turn at the second traffic light.*

3. Ele está na _____ série.

   *He's in eighth grade.*

**ANSWER KEY**
A. 1. *is open*; 2. *is at the corner*; 3. *is in the square*; 4. *who is*; 5. *where is*
B. 1. seu endereço; 2. sobrenome; 3. o segundo semáforo; 4. à direita; 5. perto daqui
C. 1. quarta; 2. segundo; 3. oitava

# ✎ Drive It Home

Translate the following sentences into English.

1. A banca de jornais é na praça.

   _____

2. O aeroporto é a quinze quilômetros daqui.

   _____

3. Vire no terceiro semáforo à esquerda.

   _____

4. Os banheiros são na segunda porta à direita.

   _____

5. Quem é o gerente?

   _____

6. Qual é o seu endereço?

   _____

7. Que carro você tem?

   _____

8. Onde é a delegacia de polícia?

   _____

**ANSWER KEY**

1. *The newsstand is in the square.* 2. *The airport is 15 kilometers from here.* 3. *Turn left at the third traffic light.* 4. *The bathrooms are on the second door to the right.* 5. *Who is the manager?* 6. *What's your address?* 7. *What car do you have?* 8. *Where is the police station?*

## Take It Further

⊳ 6H Take It Further (CD 2, Track 13)

Here's a list of common places of worship you'll find in most big cities in Brazil.

| church | igreja |
|--------|--------|
| synagogue | sinagoga |
| mosque | mesquita |
| temple | templo |

## Parting Words

Que maravilha! *Wonderful!* You've finished the lesson! How did you do? By now, you should be able to:

☐ use important vocabulary for getting around town (Still unsure? Go back to page 98.)

☐ express location and direction (Still unsure? Go back to page 98.)

☐ ask questions (Still unsure? Go back to page 99.)

☐ use ordinal numbers (Still unsure? Go back to page 100.)

☐ ask for and give directions (Still unsure? Go back to page 100.)

Don't forget to practice and reinforce what you've learned by visiting www.livinglanguage.com/languagelab for flashcards, games, and quizzes!

# Word Recall

1. How do you say *excuse me*?

   _____

2. How do you say *comfortable bed*?

   _____

3. What verb means both *there is* and *there are*?

   _____

4. How do you say *here* and *there*?

   _____

5. How do you say *the apple is red*?

   _____

6. How do you say *the apple is on the table*?

   _____

**ANSWER KEY**
1. com licença; 2. cama confortável; 3. há; 4. aqui/lá or ali; 5. a maçã é vermelha; 6. a maçã está na mesa.

# Lesson 7: Everyday Life

**Lição Sete: Cotidiano**

By the end of this lesson, you'll be able to:

☐ use regular verbs

☐ tell time

☐ talk about how often you do something

☐ use what you've learned to tell someone about your everyday life

Que horas são? *What time is it?*

## Vocabulary Builder 1

▶ 7A Vocabulary Builder 1 (CD 2, Track 14)

| | |
|---|---|
| I speak Portuguese. | Eu falo português. |
| Do you speak Italian? | Você fala italiano? |
| He speaks English. | Ele fala inglês. |
| She works a lot. | Ela trabalha muito. |
| We don't work. | Nós não trabalhamos. |
| Where do you work? | Onde você trabalha? |
| We wake up early. | Nós acordamos cedo. |
| You wake up late. | Você acorda tarde. |
| I wash the dishes. | Eu lavo a louça. |
| She waits in line. | Ela espera na fila. |
| We don't smoke. | Nós não fumamos. |
| You walk in the park. | Vocês andam no parque. |
| He has dinner alone. | Ele janta sozinho. |
| Where do you have lunch? | Onde você almoça? |
| I buy a ticket. | Eu compro um bilhete. |

## ✎ Vocabulary Practice 1

Match the Portuguese sentences with the English translation.

1. Eu falo português.       a. *You wake up late.*

2. Ela trabalha muito       b. *He speaks English.*

3. Ele fala inglês.       c. *We wake up early.*

4. Você acorda tarde.       d. *He has dinner alone.*

5. Nós acordamos cedo.       e. *I buy a ticket.*

6. Ela espera na fila.       f. *You walk in the park.*

7. Ele janta sozinho.       g. *I speak Portuguese.*

8. **Eu compro um bilhete.**

9. **Você anda no parque.**

10. **Eu lavo a louça.**

h. *I wash the dishes.*

i. *She waits in line.*

j. *She works a lot.*

**ANSWER KEY**

1. g; 2.j; 3. b; 4. a; 5. c; 6. i; 7. d; 8. e; 9. f; 10. h

# Grammar Builder 1

⊳ 7B Grammar Builder 1 (CD 2, Track 15)

## –AR VERBS

In Portuguese, most regular infinitives (the *to* form of verbs) end in –ar, –er, or –ir. Each type of infinitive follows a certain conjugation, or pattern of endings, to show agreement with a subject, like the English *I speak*, and *she speaks*. In this lesson, we'll start with the conjugation of –ar verbs such as falar (*to speak*).

| | |
|---|---|
| *I speak* | eu falo |
| *you speak* | você fala |
| *he speaks* | ele fala |
| *she speaks* | ela fala |
| *we speak* | nós falamos |
| *you speak* | vocês falam |
| *they (m.) speak* | eles falam |
| *they (f.) speak* | elas falam |

Let's see some examples. Note that the pronouns eu and nós can be dropped since the ending makes it clear who the subject is.

Estudo espanhol.
*I study Spanish.*

Estudamos matemática.
*We study math.*

**Ele não mora no Canadá.**
*He doesn't live in Canada.*

**Elas entram em casa.**
*They (f.) enter the house.*

**Vocês viajam ao Japão?**
*Do you travel to Japan?*

**O senhor chama um táxi.**
*You call a taxi.*

Here are some more common verbs ending in –ar.

| | |
|---|---|
| *to meet up, to find* | encontrar |
| *to take off or out* | tirar |
| *to make plans* | combinar |
| *to talk* | conversar |
| *to stop* | parar |
| *to look* | olhar |
| *to start* | começar |
| *to end* | terminar |
| *to send* | mandar |
| *to live* | morar |
| *to use* | usar |
| *to learn* | aprender |
| *to teach* | ensinar |
| *to visit* | visitar |
| *to put* | colocar |
| *to take someone/something* | levar |

| | |
|---|---|
| *to arrive* | chegar |
| *to listen to* | escutar |
| *to take, to have (drink/eat)* | tomar |
| *to wash* | lavar |
| *to prepare* | preparar |

## Vocabulary Builder 2

▶ 7C Vocabulary Builder 2 (CD 2, Track 16)

| | |
|---|---|
| *I work from 8:00 to 6:00.* | Eu trabalho das oito da manhã às seis da tarde. |
| *He takes a shower/bath before 7:00 a.m.* | Ele toma banho antes das sete da manhã. |
| *We arrive after midnight.* | Nós chegamos depois da meia-noite. |
| *You meet your friends at noon.* | Você encontra os seus amigos ao meio-dia. |
| *What time do they teach?* | À que horas elas ensinam? |
| *We have breakfast at 7:30.* | Tomamos café da manhã às sete e meia. |
| *He visits his parents on weekends.* | Ele visita os pais dele nos fins de semana. |
| *The supermarket closes at 10:00 p.m.* | O supermercado fecha às vinte e duas horas |
| *The bank is open from 10:00 a.m. to 4:00 p.m.* | O banco funciona das dez às dezesseis. |
| *The concert starts at 7:00 p.m.* | O concerto começa às dezenove horas. |
| *The exams end next week.* | As provas terminam na semana que vem. |

| The pilot travels three times a week. | O piloto viaja três vezes por semana. |

## ✎ Vocabulary Practice 2

Match the times.

1. oito e meia                          a. *3:45 a.m.*
2. cinco para as dez                    b. *12.30 p.m.*
3. dezessete horas e trinta minutos     c. *11:40 p.m.*
4. vinte para a meia noite              d. *9:55*
5. três e quarenta e cinco da manhã     e. *3:45 p.m.*
6. quinze para as quatro da tarde       f. *9:05*
7. nove e cinco                         g. *8:30*
8. meio-dia e meia                      h. *5:30 p.m.*

**ANSWER KEY**
1. g; 2. d; 3. h; 4. c; 5. a; 6. e; 7. f; 8. b

## Grammar Builder 2

▶ 7D Grammar Builder 2 (CD 2, Track 17)

### TELLING TIME

Que horas são? means *What time is it?*

But unlike English in which the answer always starts with *it is + hour*, in Portuguese the verb ser (*to be*) agrees with the word hora (*hour*):

é uma hora
*it's one o'clock*

são duas horas
*it's two o'clock*

Also note that **hora** is feminine so you say, **uma hora**, **duas horas**. On the other hand, **minute** (*minute*) is masculine so it's **um minuto**, **dois minutos**. Look at the examples:

**Que horas são?**
*What time is it?*

**É uma hora e dois minutos.**
*It's 1:02.*

**São duas horas e um minuto.**
*It's 2:01.*

But you don't have to use the word **minute** every time.

| | |
|---|---|
| *It's 3:05.* | **São três e cinco.** |
| *It's 4:10.* | **São quatro e dez.** |
| *It's 6:15.* | **São seis e quinze.** |
| *It's 8:30.* | **São oito e trinta.** <br> **São oito e meia. Meia** means *half (an hour)* |

Note that the following can also be said in two different ways:

| | |
|---|---|
| *It's 9:40.* | **São nove e quarenta.** <br> **São vinte para as dez.** <br> *It's twenty to ten.* |
| *It's 10:45.* | **São dez e quarenta e cinco.** <br> **São quinze para as onze.** <br> *It's fifteen to eleven.* |

Portuguese doesn't use *a.m.* or *p.m.*, instead say:

| 3:00 a.m. | São três da manhã. |
| | *It's three in the morning.* |
| 3:00 p.m. | São três da tarde. |
| | *It's three in the afternoon.* |
| 8:00 p.m. | São oito da noite. |
| | *It's eight in the evening.* |

You'll see the "military" or 24-hour time (13:00 for 1:00p.m., 14:00 for 2:00 p.m., 15.00 for 3:00p.m) for official/formal time, timetables, and schedules.

When you ask *at what time?* à que horas, there is a contraction of the article a, in a hora, with the preposition a (*at*).

À que horas é o filme? O filme é às três e meia.
*[At] what time is the movie? The movie is at three thirty.*

À que horas é a reunião? A reunião é às quinze horas.
*What time is the meeting? The meeting is at three p.m.*

Finally, to say *from 8:00 to 10:00*, you say das 8:00 às 10:00.

## Take It Further
▶ 7E Take It Further (CD 2, Track 18)

Adverbs of frequency tell you how often something occurs, as in the expression três vezes por semana (*three times a week*) which you saw above. Here are some other common adverbs of frequency.

| *always* | sempre |
| *often* | muitas vezes |

| frequently | frequentemente |
| --- | --- |
| sometimes | às vezes |
| once in a while | de vez em quando |
| rarely | raramente |
| never | nunca |

You can put these adverbs before the main verb, or at the beginning or at the end of a sentence. Look at the following examples.

| I always wear sunscreen. | Eu sempre uso protetor solar. |
| --- | --- |
| Frequently children play with dolls. | Frequentemente as crianças brincam de bonecas. |
| We often work 10 hours. | Muitas vezes trabalhamos dez horas. |
| We wake up late once in a while. | Acordamos tarde de vez em quando. |
| We sometimes eat out. | Às vezes jantamos fora. |
| He rarely buys new clothes. | Ele raramente compra roupas novas. |
| You never take vacations in the mountains. | Vocês nunca passam as férias nas montanhas. |

# ✎ Work Out 1

Complete the sentences with the appropriate adverb of frequency. The translations will guide you.

1. Os hospitais _____ fecham.

   *Hospitals never close.*

2. _____ nós acordamos ao meio-dia.

   *We wake up at noon once in a while.*

3. Os museus _____ abrem à noite.

*Museums rarely open at night.*

4. Os jovens _____ escutam música.

*Young people always listen to music.*

5. As crianças _____ estudam de manhã.

*Children frequently study in the morning.*

6. _____ os alunos chegam na hora.

*Students often arrive on time.*

7. Eu _____ chego atrasada no escritório.

*I sometimes arrive late at the office.*

8. A família viaja para o sul _____.

*The family travels south three times a year.*

**ANSWER KEY**
1. nunca; 2. de vez em quando; 3. raramente; 4. sempre; 5. frequentemente; 6. muitas vezes; 7. às vezes 8. três vezes por ano

## Bring It All Together
▶ 7F Bring It All Together (CD 2, Track 19)

**E-mail do Rio de Janeiro**

Querida mamãe,

Eu estou muito bem na faculdade aqui. Eu tenho muitos amigos e amo todos os professores!

Frequentemente, eu acordo cedo e caminho na praia durante uma hora.

Depois eu tomo o café da manhã como você sempre aconselha. As aulas são das nove da manhã às três da tarde. Eles ensinam muitas coisas interessantes!

Muitas vezes eu estudo na biblioteca das três às cinco. Duas vezes por semana, eu a minha melhor amiga, Paula, trabalhamos como voluntárias. Às vezes, quando o tempo está bom, nós jogamos vôlei na praia. No fim de semana há sempre uma festa.

Como vão o papai e a Ana? Eu mando abraços para eles e um beijo para você. Saudades,

Flávia.

*E-mail from Rio de Janeiro*

*Dear Mom,*

*I'm doing very well here in college. I have many friends and I love all the professors. Often I wake up early and take a walk on the beach for an hour. After that I have breakfast, as you always advise. Classes are from 9:00 a.m. to 3:00 p.m. They teach many interesting things! I often study in the library from 3:00 to 5:00 p.m. Twice a week, my best friend, Paula, and I work as volunteers. Once in a while when the weather is good, we play beach volleyball. On weekends there's always a party. How are Dad and Ana? I send hugs to them and a kiss to you.*

*I miss you.*

*Flavia*

## Take It Further

▶ 7G Take It Further (CD 2, Track 20)

Here are some new expressions you heard in Bring It All Together:

| I love | eu amo |
|---|---|
| I take a walk | caminho |
| for/during | durante |
| you advise | você aconselha |
| as volunteers | como voluntárias |
| the weather is fine | o tempo está bom |

| weekend | fim de semana |
|---------|---------------|
| hugs | abraços |
| a kiss | um beijo |
| I miss you | saudades |

## ✎ Work Out 2

Rewrite the following sentences in the plural, using **nós** (*we*), **vocês** (*you*), **eles** (*they, m.*), or **elas** (*they, f.*). Don't forget to change the conjugation of the verbs!

1. **Eu acordo cedo.**

   *I wake up early.*

   _____

2. **Ele trabalha muito.**

   *He works a lot.*

   _____

3. **Você não lava o carro.**

   *You don't wash the car.*

   _____

4. **Ela prepara o relatório.**

   *She prepares the report.*

   _____

5. **Você não mora na China.**

   *You don't live in China.*

6. **Eu tomo café da manhã.**

   *I have breakfast.*

7. **Ela não chega na hora.**

   *She doesn't arrive on time.*

8. **Ele escuta música.**

   *He listens to music.*

**ANSWER KEY**

1. Nós acordamos cedo. (*We wake up …* ) 2. Eles trabalham muito. (*They work …* ) 3. Vocês não lavam o carro. (*You don't wash …* ) 4. Elas preparam o relatório. (*They prepare …* ) 5. Vocês não moram na China. (*You don't live …* ) 6. Nós tomamos café da manhã. (*We have …* ) 7. Elas não chegam na hora. (*They don't arrive …* ) 8. Eles escutam música. (*They listen to …* )

## ✎ Drive It Home

Complete the following sentences with the appropriate form of the verb in parentheses. Then, translate the sentences into English.

1. Os turistas _____ um cartão postal. (mandar)

2. Maria e Pedro _____ às sete horas. (levantar)

3. Eu _____ o meu casaco. (tirar)

4. Os bancos _____ antes das quatro da tarde. (fechar)

5. Nós _____ nossos pais uma vez por semana. (visitar)

6. O meu colega _____ o ônibus às seis da tarde. (esperar)

7. Os hospitais nunca _____. (fechar)

8. A gerente _____ depois do meio-dia e meia. (almoçar)

**ANSWER KEY**

1. mandam (*The tourists send a postcard.*) 2. levantam (*Maria and Pedro get up at 7:00.*) 3. tiro (*I take off my coat.*) 4. fecham (*Banks close before 4:00 p.m.*) 5. visitamos (*We visit our parents once a week.*) 6. espera (*My colleague waits for the bus at 6:00 p.m.*) 7. fecham (*Hospitals never close.*) 8. almoça (*The manager has lunch after 12:30 p.m.*)

## Parting Words

**Perfeito!** *Perfect!* You've finished the lesson! How did you do? By now, you should be able to:

☐ use regular verbs (Still unsure? Go back to page 113.)

☐ tell time (Still unsure? Go back to page 116.)

☐ talk about how often you do something (Still unsure? Go back to page 118.)

☐ use what you've learned to tell someone about your everyday life (Still unsure? Go back to page 120.)

Don't forget to practice and reinforce what you've learned by visiting www.livinglanguage.com/languagelab for flashcards, games, and quizzes!

# Word Recall

1. What do you reply when someone says *thank you*?

   _____

2. What are the two words used for *wife*?

   _____

3. How do you say 97?

   _____

4. How do you say *pink*?

   _____

5. If o meu carro é azul means *my car is blue*, how do you say *the blue car is mine.*

   _____

6. Complete the sequence: primeiro, segundo, _____.

7. How do you say *when, where,* and *who*?

   _____

8. Say: *Sorry, I'm late.*

   _____

**ANSWER KEY**
1. de nada; 2. mulher/esposa; 3. noventa e sete; 4. cor-de-rosa; 5. o carro azul é meu; 6. terceiro; 7. quando, onde, quem; 8. Desculpe, estou atrasado(a).

# **Lesson 8:** At a Restaurant

**Lição Oito: Em um Restaurante**

By the end of this lesson, you'll be able to:

- ☐ use important vocabulary related to food
- ☐ use regular –er and –ir verbs
- ☐ say *I'd like* and *I want*
- ☐ say *this*, *that*, *these*, and *those*
- ☐ use what you've learned to order at a restaurant

**Bom apetite!** (*Enjoy your meal!*)

## Vocabulary Builder 1

▶ 8A Vocabulary Builder 1 (CD 2, Track 21)

| | |
|---|---|
| *I drink water.* | Eu bebo água. |
| *You drink beer.* | Você bebe cerveja. |
| *She doesn't drink wine.* | Ela não bebe vinho. |
| *He eats meat.* | Ele come carne. |
| *We eat fish.* | Nós comemos peixe. |
| *You eat a sandwich.* | Vocês comem um sanduíche. |
| *He orders a salad.* | Ele pede uma salada. |
| *What do you prefer?* | O que você prefere? |
| *You prefer orange juice.* | Vocês preferem suco de laranja. |
| *I prefer a lettuce and tomato salad.* | Eu prefiro uma salada de alface com tomate. |
| *We ask for the menu.* | Nós pedimos o cardápio. |
| *You call the waiter.* | Você chama o garçom. |
| *That dish looks delicious.* | Aquele prato parece delicioso. |
| *This dessert is good.* | Esta sobremesa é boa. |

## ✎ Vocabulary Practice 1

Translate the following sentences into Portuguese.

1. *I drink water.*

   _____

2. *You drink beer.*

   _____

3. *He eats meat.*

_____

4. *We eat fish.*

_____

5. *What do you prefer?*

_____

6. *You call the waiter.*

_____

7. *This dessert is good.*

_____

8. *That dish looks delicious.*

_____

**ANSWER KEY**
1. Eu bebo água. 2. Você bebe cerveja. 3. Ele come carne. 4. Nós comemos peixe. 5. O que você prefere? 6. Você chama o garçom. 7. Esta sobremesa é boa. 8. Aquele prato parece delicioso.

# Take It Further
▶ 8B Take It Further (CD 2, Track 22)

Here is some more vocabulary you can use at a restaurant.

| salt and pepper | sal e pimenta |
| bread and butter | pão e manteiga |
| toasted | torrado |
| roasted | assado |
| cooked | cozido |
| grilled | grelhado |

| | |
|---|---|
| *raw* | cru |
| *soup* | sopa |
| *legumes* | legumes |
| *vegetables* | verduras |
| *onions and garlic* | cebola e alho |
| *green beans* | vagem |
| *peas* | ervilha |
| *beans and rice* | feijão e arroz |
| *orange* | laranja |
| *lemon* | limão |
| *cherry* | cereja |
| *something you eat or drink before a meal* | aperitivo |
| *cocktail* | coquetel |

# Grammar Builder 1

▶ 8C Grammar Builder 1 (CD 2, Track 23)

## REGULAR -ER AND -IR VERBS

You've already learned that regular verbs ending in –ar are conjugated with the endings –o, –a, –amos, and –am. The second and third groups of regular verbs are verbs ending in –er and –ir respectively.

First let's see how verbs ending in –er are conjugated:

| | |
|---|---|
| *to write* | escrever |
| *I write* | eu escrevo |
| *you write* | você escreve |

| he writes | ele escreve |
| --- | --- |
| she writes | ela escreve |
| we write | nós escrevemos |
| you write | vocês escrevem |
| they write (m.) | eles escrevem |
| they write (f.) | elas escrevem |

Now let's look at –ir verbs.

| to open | abrir |
| --- | --- |
| I open | eu abro |
| you open | você abre |
| he opens | ele abre |
| she opens | ela abre |
| we open | nós abrimos |
| you open | vocês abrem |
| they open (m.) | eles abrem |
| they open (f.) | elas abrem |

Here are some common –er verbs.

| to understand | entender |
| --- | --- |
| to run | correr |
| to notice | perceber |
| to hide | esconder |
| to receive | receber |
| to die | morrer |
| to give back | devolver |
| to live | viver |
| to learn | aprender |

| *to seem/to look* | parecer |
|---|---|

Here are some common –ir verbs.

| *to watch, to attend* | assistir |
|---|---|
| *to discuss, to argue* | discutir |
| *to divide, to share* | dividir |
| *to leave, to depart* | partir |
| *to decide* | decidir |
| *to insist* | insistir |

Let's look at some examples of how to use them. To form negative sentences, put the negative **não** before the verb. To write questions, just add the question mark at the end of a written sentence, and raise the pitch when saying the sentence out loud.

**Eu escrevo uma carta.**
*I write a letter.*

**O Artur vive em Curitiba.**
*Artur lives in Curitiba.*

**Nós não recebemos o jornal em casa.**
*We don't receive (get) the paper at home.*

**Onde vocês aprendem português?**
*Where do you learn Portuguese?*

**As crianças não dividem o chocolate.**
*The children don't share the chocolate.*

A que horas parte o avião?

*What time does the plane leave?*

## Vocabulary Builder 2

▶ 8D Vocabulary Builder 2 (CD 2, Track 24)

| | |
|---|---|
| *I'd like a table for two, please.* | **Eu gostaria de uma mesa para dois, por favor.** |
| *Excuse me, could you bring the check?* | **Com licença, o senhor poderia trazer a conta?** |
| *We accept cash, check or credit card.* | **Nós aceitamos dinheiro, cheque ou cartão de crédito.** |
| *Would you like your steak well-done, medium or rare?* | **A senhora gostaria do seu filé bem passado, ao ponto ou mal passado?** |
| *Do you prefer beef or pork?* | **Os senhores preferem carne de vaca ou carne de porco?** |
| *I recommend french fries to go with that.* | **Eu recomendo batatas fritas para acompanhar.** |
| *Would you like a salad to go with that?* | **A senhora gostaria de uma salada para acompanhar?** |
| *What would you like as an appetizer?* | **O que deseja como entrada*?** |
| *This entrée/main course is typical of this region.* | **Este prato principal* é típico da região.** |
| *Excuse me, is the service included?* | **Com licença, a taxa de serviço está incluída?** |
| *Have you already decided?* | **Os senhores já escolheram?** |

* Note the false cognate: entrada means *appetizer*, whereas *entrée/main course* is prato principal.

# ✎ Vocabulary Practice 2

Translate the following expressions.

1. *excuse me* _____

2. *I'd like* _____

3. *could you* _____

4. *I recommend* _____

5. *we accept* _____

6. *already decided* _____

**ANSWER KEY**

1. **com licença**; 2. **eu gostaria**; 3. **você/o senhor/a senhora poderia**; 4. **eu recomendo**; 5. **nós aceitamos**; 6. **já escolheram**

# Take It Further

▶ 8E Take It Further (CD 2, Track 25)

You will study the verb gostar (*to like*) in a future lesson. For now note that when ordering something, use eu gostaria (*I'd like*), which is a common expression of courtesy to express desire. If you want to say how you want something done, you can use the irregular eu quero (*I want*), which is more direct. Often when someone asks you what you would like, they use o que você deseja, which literally means *what do you wish*, but is used as *what would you like* or a polite form of *what do you want*.

Que tipo de vinho o senhor deseja?
*What kind of wine would you like?*

Quero água com gás.
*I want sparkling water.*

Gostaria de reservar uma mesa para quatro pessoas, por favor.
*I'd like to make a reservation for a party of four, please.*

## Grammar Builder 2

▶ 8F Grammar Builder 2 (CD 2, Track 26)

### DEMONSTRATIVES

Demonstratives are words that point to something, like *this, that, these,* and *those* in English. Portuguese demonstratives agree in number and gender with the nouns they refer to. Just like in English, their forms vary according to distance, but three distinctions are made in Portuguese.

|                     | MASCULINE | FEMININE |
|---------------------|-----------|----------|
| *this*              | este      | esta     |
| *that*              | esse      | essa     |
| *that* (over there) | aquele    | aquela   |
| *these*             | estes     | estas    |
| *those*             | esses     | essas    |
| *those* (over there)| aqueles   | aquelas  |

The forms este(s), esta(s) refer to something that is near both the speaker and the person spoken to. They are the equivalent to *this* or *these*.

Estes guardanapos são brasileiros.
*These napkins are Brazilian.*

Nós preferimos esta mesa.
*We prefer this table.*

The forms **esse(s)** and **essa(s)** refer to something near or related to the person being spoken to, but not near the speaker. The most natural translation for this situation is *that* or *those*.

**Esse guardanapo no chão é seu?**
*Is that napkin on the floor yours?*

**Essas revistas são locais?**
*Are those local magazines?*

Finally, **aquele(s)** and **aquela(s)** refer to something that is remote or unrelated to both the speaker and the person spoken to.

**Quem é aquela mulher?**
*Who's that woman?*

**Aqueles jogadores de futebol são ótimos.**
*Those football players are great.*

Of course, sometimes you may not know what exactly you're referring to, so you won't know if it's masculine or feminine. In this case, there are neuter, invariable forms of the demonstratives: **isto** (*this thing here*), **isso** (*that thing you have there*), and **aquilo** (*that thing over there*).

**O que é isto?**
*What's this here?*

**O que é isso?**
*What's that there?*

**O que é aquilo?**
*What's that over there?*

## Take It Further

It's worth noting that in informal, spoken Brazilian Portuguese not much attention is paid to the difference between este(a) and esse(a) or isto and isso. So in spoken Portuguese, when referring to something near you can use este(a)/esse(a) or isto/isso for *this*, estes(as)/esses(as) for *these*, aquele(a), aquilo for *that* and aqueles(as) for *those*.

## ✎ Work Out 1

Translate the responses in the situations below into Portuguese.

1. Garçom: Já escolheu?

   *Waiter: Have you decided?*

   Você: _____

   *You: Yes, I'd like the chicken with green beans.*

2. Garçom: Gostaria de uma sopa como entrada?

   *Waiter: Would you like a soup to start?*

   Você: _____

   *You: No, thank you. I prefer a lettuce and tomato salad.*

3. Garçom: E para beber?

   *Waiter: And to drink?*

   Você: _____

   *You: A glass of white wine, please.*

   Garçom: Pois, não. Volto com o pão e a manteiga.

   *Waiter: Certainly, I'll return with the bread and butter.*

4. **Garçom: Gostaria de uma sobremesa?**

*Waiter: Would you like dessert?*

**Você:** _____

*You: No dessert, but some coffee. Thank you.*

**ANSWER KEY**

1. **Sim, eu gostaria de frango com vagem.** 2. **Não, eu prefiro uma salada de alface com tomate.** 3. **Uma taça de vinho branco, por favor.** 4. **Não, sobremesa não, mas sim um café. Obrigado(a).**

# Bring It All Together

▶ 8G Bring It All Together (CD 2, Track 27)

| | |
|---|---|
| *Customer:* | *Good evening. Do you have a table for one?* |
| Cliente: | **Boa noite. O senhor tem uma mesa para uma pessoa?** |
| *Waiter:* | *Yes. Come this way, please. Is this table good?* |
| Garçom: | **Pois não\*. Venha por aqui, por favor. Esta mesa está boa?** |
| *Customer:* | *Yes, thank you.* |
| Cliente: | **Sim, obrigado.** |
| *Waiter:* | *Here's the menu.* |
| Garçom: | **Aqui está o cardápio.** |
| *Customer:* | *Thank you. What typical dish do you suggest?* |
| Cliente: | **Obrigado. Que prato típico o senhor recomenda?** |
| *Waiter:* | *Today we have fish Bahia style. It's delicious.* |
| Garçom: | **Hoje, temos peixe à baiana. É delicioso!** |
| *Customer:* | *All right. I'd like the fish with french fries.* |
| Cliente: | **Está bem. Gostaria do peixe com batatas fritas.** |
| *Waiter:* | *Yes, sir. And, to drink?* |
| Garçom: | **Sim, senhor. E para beber?** |
| *Customer:* | *A very cold beer.* |
| Cliente: | **Uma cerveja bem gelada.** |
| *Waiter:* | *Excellent choice!* |
| Garçom: | **Excelente escolha!** |

* A very common Brazilian expression used by someone to signal their
willingness to assist you. It can mean *yes, certainly, of course, can I help you*, etc.

## Take It Further

▶ 8H Take It Further (CD 2, Track 28)

Here are some more useful words and phrases.

| | |
|---|---|
| *silverware: fork/knife/spoon* | **talheres: garfo/faca/colher** |
| *plate* | **prato** * |
| *glass* | **copo** |
| *bowl* | **tigela** |
| *wine glass/goblet* | **taça** |
| *white wine* | **vinho branco** |
| *red wine* | **vinho tinto** |
| *apple pie* | **torta de maçã** |
| *coconut cake* | **bolo de coco** |
| *mashed potatoes* | **purê de batatas** |
| *individual portion* | **porção individual** |
| *appetizer portion* | **porção aperitivo** |
| *table cloth* | **toalha de mesa** |
| *waiting list* | **lista de espera** |

* Note the different meanings for **prato**: **prato principal** means *main course*, **prato(s)** means
*plate(s)*, and in the plural **pratos** also means *dishes* in general.

**Para o prato principal, eu recomendo o frango.**
*For the main course, I recommend the chicken.*

**Este prato é de porcelana francesa.**
*This is plate is made of French porcelain.*

**Lave os pratos!**
*Wash the dishes!*

---

## ✎ Work Out 2

Let's practice with the three regular endings you've learned. Put the verbs in parentheses in the appropriate form.

1. **Você _____ esta palavra? (entender)**

   *Do you understand this word?*

2. **O que vocês _____ para acompanhar a carne? (escolher)**

   *What do you choose to go with the meat?*

3. **Ana e Paulo _____ uma mesa para duas pessoas. (esperar)**

   *Ana and Paulo wait for a table for two.*

4. **As amigas _____ a sobremesa. (dividir)**

   *The friends share the dessert.*

5. **Eu _____ cedo. (partir)**

   *I leave early.*

6. **Esse restaurante _____ ser muito bom. (parecer)**

   *This restaurant seems to be very good.*

7. **A máquina de lavar pratos _____ todos os pratos, copos e talheres.**

   **(lavar)**

   *The dishwasher washes all the dishes, glasses and silverware.*

8. **O meu amigo** _____ **um restaurante típico brasileiro.**

   **(recomendar)**

   *My friend recommends a typical Brazilian restaurant.*

9. **O meu marido e eu** _____ **nossos amigos para jantar.**

   **(receber)**

   *My husband and I have our friends over for dinner.*

**ANSWER KEY**

1. entende; 2. escolhem; 3. esperam; 4. dividem; 5. parto; 6. parece; 7. lava; 8. recomenda; 9. recebemos

# Take It Further

▶ 8I Take It Further (CD 2, Track 29)

The regular verb **tomar** means *to take*. **Tome uma aspirina** means *take an aspirin*. However, it can also mean *to have* when this refers to eating or drinking something. Look at the following examples:

**Ele toma café com leite.**
*He has coffee with milk.*

**Nós tomamos sopa de cebola.**
*We have onion soup.*

**Eu gostaria de tomar um sorvete de morango.**
*I'd like to have strawberry ice cream.*

# ✎ Drive It Home

A. Complete the following sentences with a demonstrative: este/esta/estes/estas, aquele/aquela/aqueles/aquelas.

1. Eu prefiro _____ sapatos aqui.

   *I prefer these shoes here.*

2. João, _____ clientes lá perto da porta não receberam o

   cardápio.

   *Joao, those customers over there near the door didn't get a menu.*

3. _____ carta é para a senhora.

   *This letter is for you, ma'am.*

4. Senhor, _____ bananas aqui estão boas para hoje?

   *Sir, are these bananas here good for today?*

5. _____ café é seu porque não tem açúcar.

   *This is your coffee because it has no sugar.*

6. Quem são _____ pessoas na sala do gerente?

   *Who are those people in the manager's office?*

7. Ah, Paris! _____ cidade é muito romântica!

   *Ah, Paris! That city is very romantic!*

8. Não, este aqui não é o meu casaco. O meu casaco é _____ lá.

   *No, this here is not my coat. My coat is that one over there.*

B. Now, complete these sentences with one of the following: isto /aquilo

1. **Você entende o que é** _____ **aqui?**

   *Do you understand what this is here?*

2. **O que é** _____ **na televisão?**

   *What's that on TV?*

3. **Com licença,** _____ **aqui é seu?**

   *Excuse me, is this yours?*

4. _____ **do outro lado da rua é uma loja ou um restaurante?**

   *That on the other side of the street is a store or a restaurant?*

   **ANSWER KEY**

   A. 1. estes; 2. aqueles; 3. Esta; 4. estas; 5. Este; 6. aquelas; 7. Aquela; 8. aquele;
   B. 1. isto; 2. aquilo; 3. isto; 4. Aquilo

## Parting Words

**Bom trabalho!** *Well done!* You've finished the lesson! How did you do? You should now be able to:

☐ use important vocabulary related to food (Still unsure? Go back to page 127.)

☐ use regular –er and –ir verbs (Still unsure? Go back to page 129.)

☐ say *I'd like* and *I want* (Still unsure? Go back to page 132.)

☐ say *this*, *that*, *these*, and *those* (Still unsure? Go back to page 134.)

☐ use what you've learned to order at a restaurant (Still unsure? Go back to page 137.)

Don't forget to practice and reinforce what you've learned by visiting www.livinglanguage.com/languagelab for flashcards, games, and quizzes!

# Word Recall

Translate the following sentences into Portuguese.

1. *The pleasure is mine.*

   _____

2. *I want to introduce my family.*

   _____

3. *I have a headache.*

   _____

4. *She's sleepy.*

   _____

5. *The sea is very blue.*

   _____

6. *There's an ATM next to the pharmacy.*

   _____

7. *Classes are from 9:00 a.m. to 3:00 p.m.*

   _____

8. *What typical dish do you suggest?*

   _____

**ANSWER KEY**
1. O prazer é meu. 2. Quero apresentar a minha família. 3. Eu tenho dor de cabeça. 4. Ela está com sono. 5. O mar é muito azul. 6. Há um caixa eletrônico ao lado da farmácia. 7. As aulas são das nove da manhã às três da tarde. 8. Que prato típico o senhor recomenda?

# Lesson 9: At Work

## Lição Nove: No Trabalho

By the end of this lesson, you'll be able to:

☐ name common professions

☐ use the verb **ir** (*to go*)

☐ use the verb **fazer** (*to do/to make*)

☐ say the days of the week and months of the year

☐ use what you've learned to talk about your job

**Vamos trabalhar!** *Let's get to work!*

## Vocabulary Builder 1

9A Vocabulary Builder 1 (CD 2, Track 30)

| Programmers program computers. | Programadores programam computadores. |
|---|---|
| Veterinarians treat animals. | Veterinários cuidam de animais. |
| Pilots fly airplanes. | Pilotos voam aviões. |
| Lawyers defend clients. | Advogados defendem clientes. |
| Actors rehearse plays. | Atores ensaiam peças de teatro. |
| Journalists interview politicians. | Jornalistas entrevistam políticos. |
| Directors direct companies. | Diretores dirigem companhias. |
| Writers write novels. | Escritores escrevem romances. |
| Cooks make food. | Cozinheiros fazem comida. |
| Salespeople sell products. | Vendedores vendem produtos. |
| Janitors clean offices. | Faxineiros fazem faxina em escritórios. |
| Teachers give lessons. | Professores dão aulas. |

## Vocabulary Practice 1

Match the verbs and the professions. Use the translation to help you.

1. Atores _____  a. voam peças de teatro.
   Actors rehearse plays.

2. Diretores _____  b. entrevistam companhias.
   Directors direct companies.

3. Pilotos _____  c. ensaiam aviões.
   Pilots fly airplanes.

4. Advogados _____  d. dão clientes.
   Lawyers defend clients.

5. **Professores** _____ e. **dirigem aula.**
   *Teachers give lessons.*

6. **Cozinheiros** _____ f. **defendem comida.**
   *Cooks make food.*

7. **Veterinários** _____ g. **cuidam de animais.**
   *Veterinarians treat animals.*

8. **Jornalistas** _____ h. **programam políticos.**
   *Journalists interview politicians.*

9. **Vendedores** _____ i. **fazem produtos.**
   *Salespeople sell products.*

10. **Programadores** _____ j. **vendem computadores.**
   *Programmers program computers.*

**ANSWER KEY**
1. c; 2. e; 3. a; 4. f. 5. d; 6. i; 7. g; 8.b; 9. j; 10. h

# Grammar Builder 1
▶ 9B Grammar Builder 1 (CD 2, Track 31)

**THE IRREGULAR VERB IR (*TO GO*) AND CONTRACTIONS WITH A (*TO*)**

The irregular verb ir means *to go.*

| *I go* | eu vou |
|---|---|
| *you go* | você vai |
| *he/she goes* | ele/ela vai |
| *we go* | nós vamos |
| *you go* | vocês vão |
| *they go* | eles/elas vão |

**Eu vou à escola.**
*I go to school.*

**Onde nós vamos?**
*Where are we going?*

**Elas não vão ao aeroporto. Elas vão à estação rodoviária.**
*They're not going to the airport. They're going to the bus station.*

Just as in English, the verb ir is often followed by the preposition a (*to*). A forms a contraction with the definite article, much like other prepositions you've already seen, such as de and em. Notice the grave accent in the feminine forms.

| a + o = ao | a + os = os |
|---|---|
| a + a = à | a + as = às |

**Ele vai à praia de Copacabana.**
*He's going to Copacabana beach.*

**Elas vão ao circo.**
*They're going to the circus.*

**Nós vamos ao jogo de futebol.**
*We're going to the soccer game.*

**Você vai às festas de fim de ano.**
*You are going to the holiday parties.*

Just as in English, you can express the future with ir:

**Eu vou acordar cedo.**
*I'm going to wake up early.*

**Onde você vai passar as férias?**
*Where are you going to spend your vacation?*

**Eles vão chegar na hora?**
*Are they going to arrive on time?*

**A empresa não vai dar um aumento.**
*The company isn't going to give a raise.*

**O professor vai dar uma prova amanhã.**
*The teacher is going to give a test tomorrow.*

## Vocabulary Builder 2

▶ 9C Vocabulary Builder 2 (CD 2, Track 32)

| | |
|---|---|
| *I'm going to take a business trip.* | **Vou fazer uma viagem de negócios.** |
| *My company is going to invest more.* | **A minha empresa vai investir mais.** |
| *Our meeting is going to be put off.* | **A nossa reunião vai ser adiada.** |
| *The workers are going to go on strike.* | **Os trabalhadores vão entrar em greve.** |
| *The assistant is not going to work tomorrow.* | **A assistente não vai trabalhar amanhã.** |
| *We're going to deliver the project.* | **Nós vamos entregar o projeto.** |
| *When are you going to take vacations?* | **Quando você vai tirar férias?** |
| *The manager is going to schedule a meeting.* | **A gerente vai marcar uma reunião.** |
| *They're going to do business with China.* | **Eles vão fazer negócios com a China.** |
| *The firm is going to pay a bonus.* | **A firma vai pagar um bônus.** |

| *I'm going to take the day off.* | **Eu vou tirar o dia de folga.** |
| *He's going to take a medical leave.* | **Ele vai tirar licença médica.** |

# ✎ Vocabulary Practice 2

A. Translate the following into English.

1. **tirar o dia de folga** _____

2. **tirar licença médica** _____

3. **marcar uma reunião** _____

4. **entrar em greve** _____

B. Now, translate these phrases into Portuguese:

1. *to pay a bonus* _____

2. *to deliver the project* _____

3. *to be put off* _____

4. *to take a business trip* _____

5. *to do business* _____

**ANSWER KEY**
A. 1. *take the day off*; 2. *take a medical leave*; 3. *to schedule a meeting*; 4. *to go on strike*;
B. 5. **pagar um bônus**; 6. **entregar o projeto**; 7. **ser adiado**; 8. **fazer uma viagem de negócios**; 9. **fazer negócios**

## Take It Further

▶ 9D Take It Further 1 (CD 2, Track 33)

The irregular verb **fazer** means *to do* or *to make*. First let's look at how it is conjugated:

| | |
|---|---|
| *I do/make* | eu faço |
| *you do/make* | você faz |
| *he/she does/makes* | ele/ela faz |
| *we do/make* | nós fazemos |
| *you do/make* | vocês fazem |
| *they do/make* | eles/elas fazem |

Now look at some examples of how it is used.

**Eu faço a minha lição de casa.**
*I do my homework.*

**Vocês fazem negócios na China?**
*Do you do business in China?*

**Quem fez aquilo?**
*Who did that?* or *Who made that?*

**Minha amiga faz um bolo delicioso.**
*My friend makes a delicious cake.*

# Grammar Builder 2

▶ 9E Grammar Builder 2 (CD 3, Track 1)

## DAYS, DATES, AND PREPOSITIONS OF TIME

First let's learn the days of the week and months of the year.

| days of the week | dias da semana |
|---|---|
| Monday | segunda-feira |
| Tuesday | terça-feira |
| Wednesday | quarta-feira |
| Thursday | quinta-feira |
| Friday | sexta-feira |
| Saturday | sábado |
| Sunday | domingo |

Note that the days of the week are not capitalized. Also the word feira is optional in spoken Portuguese. If you want to say that something happens on a particular day, use no (*on the*) for sábado and domingo, which are masculine, and na (*on the*) for the other days, which are feminine.

Eu chego no domingo.
*I arrive on Sunday.*

Ele parte na sexta-feira.
*He leaves on Friday.*

When you want to say that something happens in general, for example *on Mondays*, use aos (sábado and domingo) and às (for *Monday–Friday*):

Nós assistimos televisão aos domingos.
*We watch TV on Sundays.*

Ela faz ginástica às segundas e quartas.
*She works out on Mondays and Wednesdays.*

Now, let's look at os meses do ano (*the months of the year*), which are also not capitalized.

| January | janeiro |
|---------|---------|
| February | fevereiro |
| March | março |
| April | abril |
| May | maio |
| June | junho |
| July | julho |
| August | agosto |
| September | setembro |
| October | outubro |
| November | novembro |
| December | dezembro |

If you want to say that something happens in a particular month, use the preposition em:

No Brasil o inverno começa em junho.
*In Brazil winter starts in June.*

Primavera means *spring* and is feminine. The other seasons, which are masculine, are verão, outono and inverno (*summer, fall,* and *winter*).

If you want to say that something happens in a particular season, use the preposition na for primavera and no for the others.

**As praias estão cheias no verão.**
*The beaches are crowded in summer.*

**Minhas aulas terminam na primavera.**
*My classes end in spring.*

## Take It Further

▶ 9F Take It Further (CD 3, Track 2)

In the vocabulary list, you saw the expression fazer negócios (*to do business*), now let's look at some other common expressions using the verb fazer (*to do/to make*).

| It doesn't matter. | Não faz mal. |
|---|---|
| to make friends | fazer amigos |
| to turn xx years old | fazer xx anos |
| to be nice (weather) | fazer tempo bom |
| to go shopping | fazer compras |

## ✎ Work Out 1

Complete the following sentences with the correct form of the verb ir and one verb from the box below to form sentences in the immediate future.

trabalhar, viajar, fazer, pedir, investir, ficar, aprender, dar

1. **A gerente** _____ **uma viagem de negócios.**

   *The manager is going to take a business trip.*

2. **A minha família** _____ **para a praia em janeiro.**

   *My family is going to travel to the beach in January.*

3. Nós _____ nosso dinheiro naquele banco.

   *We're going to invest our money in that bank.*

4. Os trabalhadores _____ um aumento.

   *The workers are going to ask for a raise.*

5. Mariana e Pedro _____ duas noites no Hotel Ipanema.

   *Mariana and Pedro are going to spend two nights at the Ipanema Hotel.*

6. O professor _____ aulas na segunda-feira?

   *Is the teacher going to give classes on Monday?*

7. Eu _____ português no Brasil.

   *I'm going to learn Portuguese in Brazil.*

8. Vocês não _____ aos sábados ou domingos.

   *You're not going to work on Saturdays or Sundays.*

   **ANSWER KEY**
   1. vai fazer; 2. vai viajar; 3. vamos investir; 4. vão pedir; 5. vão ficar; 6. vai dar; 7. vou aprender; 8. vão trabalhar

## Bring It All Together
▶ 9G Bring It All Together (CD 3, Track 3)

| | |
|---|---|
| *Manager:* | *Good morning! How's everything? How's my agenda for today?* |
| Gerente: | Bom dia! Tudo bem? Como está a minha agenda para hoje? |
| *Assistant:* | *Your agenda is jam-packed!* |
| Assistente: | Sua agenda está lotada! |
| *Manager:* | *What's the first activity of the day?* |
| Gerente: | Qual é a primeira atividade do dia? |
| *Assistant:* | *The meeting with Mr. Joao Carlos and Ms. Vitoria.* |
| Assistente: | A reunião com o Sr. João Carlos e a Sra. Vitória. |

| | |
|---|---|
| *Manager:* | *I'm going to use the sales presentation. Is it ready?* |
| **Gerente:** | **Vou usar a apresentação de vendas. Ela está pronta?** |
| *Assistant:* | *Yes, it is. The meeting is from 9:00 to 10:30.* |
| **Assistente:** | **Está sim. A reunião vai das nove às dez e meia.** |
| *Manager:* | *And after that?* |
| **Gerente:** | **E depois?** |
| *Assistant:* | *After that we're going to have a visit from the production director.* |
| **Assistente:** | **Depois vamos ter a visita da diretora de produção.** |
| *Manager:* | *Am I going to have a business lunch today?* |
| **Gerente:** | **Vou ter almoço de negócios hoje?** |
| *Assistant:* | *No, not today.* |
| **Assistente:** | **Não, hoje não.** |
| *Manager:* | *That's fortunate!* |
| **Gerente:** | **Que sorte!** |
| *Assistant:* | *Yes, but the afternoon is going to be one meeting after the other until 7:00p.m.!* |
| **Assistente:** | **É, mas a tarde vai ser uma reunião depois da outra até as dezenove horas!** |
| *Manager:* | *It doesn't matter! Tomorrow is Saturday and we're not going to work!* |
| **Gerente:** | **Não faz mal. Amanhã é sábado e nós não vamos trabalhar!** |

# ✎ Work Out 2

1. Write the days of the week, starting with *Monday*.


2. Write the months of the year in Portuguese.


**ANSWER KEY**

1. segunda-feira, terça-feira, quarta-feira, quinta-feira, sexta-feira, sábado, domingo; 2. janeiro, fevereiro, março, abril, maio, junho, julho, agosto, setembro, outubro, novembro, dezembro

# ✎ Drive It Home

Match the sentence in Column A with a verb from Column B and a profession from Column C.

| Column A | Column B | Column C |
|---|---|---|

**Column A**

1. **Eu vou** _____
   **de gatos e cachorros.**
   *I'm going to treat cats and dogs.*

2. **Ele vai** _____
   **um cliente.**
   *He's going to defend a client.*

3. **Ela vai** _____
   **uma reunião.**
   *She's going to direct a meeting.*

4. **Eles vão** _____
   **dez escritórios.**
   *They're going to clean ten offices.*

5. **Eles vão** _____
   **uma peça de teatro.**
   *They're going to rehearse a play.*

6. **Eu vou** _____
   **um Boeing 707.**
   *I'm going to fly a Boeing 707.*

7. **Ela vai** _____
   **um romance.**
   *She's going to write a novel.*

8. **Ele vai** _____
   **um jantar para vinte pessoas.**
   *He's going to cook a dinner for twenty people.*

**Column B**

a. limpar

b. tratar

c. fazer

d. escrever

e. defender

f. ensaiar

g. voar

h. dirigir

**Column C**

i. advogado

j. veterinário

k. faxineiros

l. cozinheiro

m. atores

n. escritor

o. piloto

p. diretor

**ANSWER KEY**
1. b/j; 2. e/i; 3. h/p; 4. a/k; 5. f/m; 6. g/o; 7. d/n; 8. c/l

# Parting Words

Ótimo! *Great!* You've finished Lesson 9! How did you do? By now, you should be able to:

☐ identify some professional activities (Still unsure? Go back to page 145.)

☐ use the verb ir *(to go)* (Still unsure? Go back to page 146.)

☐ use the verb fazer *(to do /to make)* (Still unsure? Go back to page 150.)

☐ say the days of the weeks and dates (Still unsure? Go back to page 151.)

☐ use what you've learned to talk about your job (Still unsure? Go back to page 154.)

Don't forget to practice and reinforce what you've learned by visiting www.livinglanguage.com/languagelab for flashcards, games, and quizzes!

# Word Recall

Put the following Portuguese verbs in the infinitive and then translate into English.

1. sou _____

2. estamos _____

3. faz _____

4. gostaria _____

5. tenho _____

6. viram _____

7. chamam _____

8. aprende _____

9. abre _____

10. vão _____

**ANSWER KEY**
1. ser, *to be*; 2. estar, *to be*; 3. fazer, *to do/to make*; 4. gostar, *to like*; 5. ter, *to have*; 6. virar, *to turn/to become*; 7. chamar, *to call*; 8. aprender, *to learn*; 9. abrir, *to open*; 10. ir, *to go*

Essential Brazilian Portuguese

# Lesson 10: Among Friends

**Lição Dez: Entre Amigos**

By the end of this lesson, you'll be able to:

☐ use the verb *gostar de* (*to like*)

☐ use some common irregular verbs

☐ use the verbs *querer* (*to want*) and *poder* (*can*)

☐ use what you've learned to talk about socializing and entertaining

**Que divertido!** *What fun!*

## Vocabulary Builder 1

▶ 10A Vocabulary Builder 1 (CD 3, Track 4)

| | |
|---|---|
| *I like to ride bicycles.* | **Eu gosto de andar de bicicleta.** |
| *Do you like soccer?* | **Você gosta de futebol?** |
| *Children don't like to sleep.* | **As crianças não gostam de dormir.** |
| *I like your car.* | **Eu gosto do seu carro.** |
| *We like your house.* | **Nós gostamos da sua casa.** |
| *Who likes pizza?* | **Quem gosta de pizza?** |
| *He doesn't like to play tennis.* | **Ele não gosta de jogar tênis.** |
| *She loves carnival.* | **Ela adora o carnaval.** |
| *I hate traffic.* | **Eu detesto trânsito.** |
| *Don't you hate lines?* | **Você não odeia filas?** |
| *How about you? What do you like to do?* | **E você? O que você gosta de fazer?** |
| *Do you prefer to play or watch sports?* | **Você prefere jogar ou assistir esportes?** |
| *What kind of movies do you like?* | **Que tipo de filme você gosta?** |
| *Who's your favorite singer?* | **Quem é o seu cantor predileto?** |

## ✎ Vocabulary Practice 1

Match the phrases in Column A with their translations in Column B.

1. gostamos da sua casa
2. gosto de andar de bicicleta
3. odeia filas
4. gosto do seu carro
5. adora o carnaval
6. prefere jogar

a. *prefers to play*
b. *favorite singer*
c. *hate traffic*
d. *don't like to sleep*
e. *who likes*
f. *like to ride a bicycle*

7. cantor favorito

8. não gostam de dormir

9. quem gosta de

10. detesto trânsito

g. *like your house*

h. *hate lines*

i. *loves carnival*

j. *like your car*

**ANSWER KEY**

1. g; 2. f; 3. h; 4. j; 5. i; 6. a; 7. b; 8. d; 9. e; 10. c

# Grammar Builder 1

10B Grammar Builder 1 (CD 3, Track 5)

## THE VERB GOSTAR DE (*TO LIKE*)

The regular verb gostar is used to talk about things you *like*, or in the negative, things you *dislike*. Gostar is conjugated as a regular –ar verb:

| I like | eu gosto |
|---|---|
| you like | você gosta |
| he/she likes | ele/ela gosta |
| we like | nós gostamos |
| you like | vocês gostam |
| they like | eles/elas gostam |

The thing that is liked or disliked is always introduced by the preposition de. That can be a noun or a verb.

Eu gosto de cerveja.

*I like beer.*

Eu gosto de tomar cerveja.

*I like to drink beer.*

**Eu não gosto de filmes violentos.**
*I don't like violent movies.*

**Eu não gosto de assistir filmes violentos.**
*I don't like to watch violent movies.*

In the examples above, you're talking about things you like or dislike in general.

When you want to talk about specific things you like or dislike, you have to use the preposition de contracted with the definite articles o, a, os, as.

| SINGULAR | PLURAL |
|---|---|
| de + o = do | de + os = dos |
| de + a = da | de + as = das |

Compare these two sentences:

**Ele gosta de gatos.**
*He likes cats.*

**Ele gosta do gato dele.**
*He likes his cat.*

Look at some more examples of how to use gostar de to talk about specific likes or dislikes.

**Você gosta da amiga da Carol?**
*Do you like Carol's friend?*

**Nós não gostamos das fotos.**
*We don't like the photos.*

**Vocês gostam dos planos para as férias?**

*Do you like the vacation plans?*

## Take It Further

Let's look at three common irregular verbs in the present. First see how they're conjugated.

### LER *(TO READ)*

| I read | eu leio |
|---|---|
| you read | você lê |
| he/she reads | ele/ela lê |
| we read | nós lemos |
| you read | vocês leem |
| they read | eles/elas leem |

### VIR *(TO COME)*

| I come | eu venho |
|---|---|
| you come | você vem |
| he/she comes | ele/ela vem |
| we come | nós vimos |
| you come | vocês vêm |
| they come | eles/elas vêm |

### DAR *(TO GIVE)*

| I give | eu dou |
|---|---|

| you give | você dá |
|----------|---------|
| he/she gives | ele/ela dá |
| we give | nós damos |
| you give | vocês dão |
| they give | eles/elas dão |

Now, look at some examples of how to use these irregular verbs.

**Eu leio romances e biografias.**
*I read novels and biographies.*

**Nós não lemos o jornal todos os dias.**
*We don't read the newspaper every day.*

**O Pedro e a Cecília vêm jantar em casa.**
*Pedro and Cecilia are coming over for dinner.*

**A que horas você vem aqui?**
*What time are you coming here?*

**Quando vocês dão jantares em casa?**
*When do you give dinner parties at home?*

**Paula dá dinheiro para caridade.**
*Paula gives money to charity.*

## Vocabulary Builder 2

▶ 10C Vocabulary Builder 2 (CD 3, Track 6)

| | |
|---|---|
| I want to rest. | Eu quero descansar. |
| She wants to swim. | Ela quer nadar. |
| Do you want to go to a party? | Você quer ir a uma festa? |
| When do you want to travel? | Quando vocês querem viajar? |
| We want two tickets. | Nós queremos dois ingressos. |
| I can have dinner on Saturday. | Eu posso jantar no sábado. |
| When can you go out? | Quando você pode sair? |
| They can't come to the opening. | Eles não podem vir à inauguração. |
| She can play the piano. | Ela pode tocar piano. |
| Can you reserve three places? | Vocês podem reservar três lugares? |
| Can I walk there? | Eu posso ir lá a pé? |
| Do you want to go out with me? | Você quer sair comigo? |

## Take It Further

The irregular verb sair means *to leave, to get out* or *to go out*. First, let's see how it's conjugated, and then let's see some examples of how it's used to convey different meanings.

| | |
|---|---|
| I leave/go out | eu saio |
| you leave/go out | você sai |
| he/she leaves/goes out | ele/ela sai |
| we leave/go out | nós saímos |
| you leave/go out | vocês saem |
| they leave/go out | eles/elas saem |

**Que horas sai o trem para Belo Horizonte?**
*What time does the train to Belo Horizonte leave?*

**Vocês saem do trabalho às cinco ou às seis da tarde?**
*Do you leave work at 5 or 6 p.m.?*

**A Paula e o Pedro saem juntos.**
*Paula and Pedro go out together.*

**Aos domingos eu saio com meus amigos.**
*On Sundays, I go out with my friends.*

**Vamos sair de casa e ir ao cinema!**
*Let's get out of the house and go to the movies!*

**Saia do meu lugar!**
*Get out of my seat [lit. place]!*

---

# ✎ Vocabulary Practice 2

A. Translate the following phrases into English.

1. Você quer ir a uma festa?

_____

2. Quando vocês querem viajar?

_____

3. Quando você pode sair?

_____

4. Vocês podem reservar três lugares?

5. Eles não podem vir à inauguração.

B. Now, translate the following sentences into Portuguese.

1. *I want to rest.*

2. *She wants to swim.*

3. *We want two tickets.*

4. *She can play the piano.*

5. *Can I walk there?*

**ANSWER KEY**

A. 1. *Do you want to go to a party?* 2. *When do you want to travel?* 3. *When can you go out?* 4. *Can you reserve three seats [lit. places]?* 5. *They can't come to the opening.*

B. 6. Eu quero descansar. 7. Ela quer nadar. 8. Nós queremos dois ingressos. 9. Ela pode tocar piano. 10. Eu posso ir lá a pé?

## Take It Further

The words ingresso and entrada mean *ticket* when referring to um filme (*a movie*), um concerto (*a classical music concert*), um show (*a rock concert*), um jogo (*a game*), or uma peça (*a play*).

Nós queremos dois ingressos para a sessão das dezenove horas, por favor.
*We want two tickets for the 7:00 p.m. show, please.*

Eu gostaria de uma entrada para o show das dezenove e trinta.
*I'd like a ticket for the 7:30 pm show.*

You should use bilhete or passagem when referring to a ticket for a means of transportation. So you'd say bilhete/passagem de avião (*plane ticket*), bilhete/passagem de trem (*train ticket*), or bilhete/passagem de ônibus (*bus ticket*).

Eu gostaria de uma passagem para o trem das vinte horas para o Rio de Janeiro, por favor.
*I'd like a ticket for the 8:00 p.m. train to Rio de Janeiro, please.*

O nosso bilhete de avião está na minha bolsa.
*Our airplane ticket is in my handbag.*

## Grammar Builder 2

▶ 10D Grammar Builder 2 (CD 3, Track 7)

### QUERER (*TO WANT*) AND PODER (*CAN*)

The irregular verb querer means *to want*, and just like in English it is followed by a noun or a verb in the infinitive.

First, let's see how it's conjugated:

| I want | eu quero |
|--------|----------|
| you want | você quer |
| he/she wants | ele/ela quer |
| we want | nós queremos |
| you want | vocês querem |
| they want | eles/elas querem |

Now, let's study some examples of how to use it.

Eu quero um ingresso para o jogo de tênis.
*I want a ticket for the tennis game.*

Nós queremos viajar de navio.
*We want to travel by ship.*

O que você quer para o café da manhã?
*What do you want for breakfast?*

The irregular verb poder means *can* or *to be able to* and is also followed by a verb in the infinitive. Look at how it's conjugated.

| I can | eu posso |
|-------|----------|
| you can | você pode |
| he/she can | ele/ela pode |
| we can | nós podemos |
| you can | vocês podem |
| they can | eles/elas podem |

Note that just as in English, poder has two different meanings. One meaning for poder is *to have the ability* or *skill*, as in eu posso tocar piano (*I can play the piano.*) The other meaning is *to be possible* as in eu posso ir ao cinema amanhã (*I can go to the movies tomorrow.*)

Look at some more examples.

Eles não podem correr a maratona.
*They can't run the marathon.*

Você pode esquiar?
*Can you ski?*

Os meus amigos não podem vir no domingo.
*My friends can't come on Sunday.*

Que horas você pode sair na sexta-feira?
*What time can you go out on Friday?*

## ✎ Work Out 1

Unscramble the following sentences:

1. Eu/esquiar/de/no/gosto/inverno

   *I like to ski in winter.*

   _____

2. gostam/Elas/nadar/de/no/não/mar

   *They don't like to swim in the sea.*

   _____

3. gostam/horas/aos/vocês/de/sábados/acordar/Que

*What time do you like to wake up on Saturdays?*

4. praia/você/Quando/ir/de/gosta/à

*When do you like to go to the beach?*

5. tarde/Nós/de/gostamos/não/jantar

*We don't like to have dinner late.*

6. tipo/Que/comida/de/gostam/vocês

*What kind of food do you like?*

7. futebol/gosta/filho/de/jogar/Meu

*My son likes to play soccer.*

8. de/descansar/domingos/em/casa/gosto/aos/Eu

*I like to rest at home on Sundays.*

**ANSWER KEY**

1. Eu gosto de esquiar no inverno. 2. Elas não gostam de nadar no mar. 3. Que horas vocês gostam de acordar aos sábados? 4. Quando você gosta de ir à praia? 5. Nós não gostamos de jantar tarde. 6. Que tipo de comida vocês gostam? 7. Meu filho gosta de jogar futebol. 8. Eu gosto de descansar em casa aos domingos.

# ◖ Bring It All Together

▷ 10E Bring It All Together (CD 3, Track 8)

| | |
|---|---|
| *Sandra:* | *Do you like action movies?* |
| Sandra: | Você gosta de filmes de ação? |
| *Carlos:* | *Sometimes, but I prefer old movies like Casablanca.* |
| Carlos: | Às vezes, mas prefiro filmes antigos como Casablanca. |
| *Sandra:* | *Cool! Me too! I love Humphrey Bogart. He's my favorite actor!* |
| Sandra: | Que legal! Eu também. Eu amo Humphrey Bogart. Ele é o meu ator favorito! |
| *Carlos:* | *And the theater? Do you go to the theater?* |
| Carlos: | E teatro? Você vai ao teatro? |
| *Sandra:* | *Yes, I do, but not a lot because it's expensive.* |
| Sandra: | Sim vou, mas não muito porque é caro. |
| *Carlos:* | *I agree, especially for students like us.* |
| Carlos: | Concordo, principalmente para estudantes como nós. |
| *Sandra:* | *Do you like to travel?* |
| Sandra: | Você gosta de viajar? |
| *Carlos:* | *I love to travel. But I don't like to go to the beach on Sundays because I hate traffic. What about you?* |
| Carlos: | Adoro viajar. Mas não gosto de ir à praia aos domingos porque odeio o trânsito. E você? |
| *Sandra:* | *I prefer to stay in the city on Sundays. I can study and read.* |
| Sandra: | Eu prefiro ficar na cidade aos domingos. Eu posso estudar e ler. |
| *Carlos:* | *Let's go to the movies later? We can watch a black and white movie.* |
| Carlos: | Vamos ao cinema mais tarde? Podemos assistir a um filme preto e branco. |
| *Sandra:* | *Of course, let's go!* |
| Sandra: | Claro, vamos! |

# ✎ Work Out 2

Make the following sentences more formal/polite. Remember to use either o senhor or a senhora in place of você and os senhores or as senhoras instead of vocês.

1. Eu quero sorvete de chocolate.

   *I want chocolate ice-cream.*

2. Você quer um ingresso para o filme das nove?

   *Do you want a ticket for the 9 o'clock show?*

3. Nós queremos uma mesa para dois.

   *We want a table for two.*

4. Ana e Paulo, vocês podem vir à reunião?

   *Ana and Paulo, can you come to the meeting?*

5. João, que horas você pode telefonar?

   *João, what time can you call?*

6. Eu posso abrir a janela?

   *Can I open the window?*

7. **Helena, você pode vir aqui?**

   *Helen, can you come here?*

8. **José e Carlos, vocês podem trabalhar até as vinte horas?**

   *Jose and Carlos, can you work until 8:00 p.m.?*

**ANSWER KEY**

1. Eu queria um sorvete de chocolate. or Eu gostaria de um ... (*I'd like a chocolate ice-cream.*) 2. Você queria um ingresso para o filme das nove? or Você gostaria de um ingresso ... (*Would you like a ticket for the 9:00 show?*) 3. Nós queríamos uma mesa para dois. or Nós gostaríamos de uma ... (*We'd like a table for two.*) 4. Sra. Ana e Sr. Paulo, os senhores poderiam vir à reunião? (*Ms. Ana and Mr. Paulo, could you come to the meeting?*) 5. Sr. João, que horas o senhor poderia telefonar? (*Mr. João, what time could you call?*) 6. Eu poderia abrir a janela? (*Could I open the window?*) 7. Sra. Helena, a senhora poderia vir aqui? (*Ms. Helena, could you come here?*) 8. Sr. José e Sr. Carlos, os senhores poderiam trabalhar até as vinte horas? (*Messrs. Jose and Carlos, could you work until 8:00 p.m.?*)

## Take It Further

You already saw that you can use the verb gostar de followed by a noun or a verb to talk about things you like in general: eu gosto de maçãs (*I like apples*); and with the contractions da, do, das, dos to talk about specific things you like: eu gosto da torta de maçã da minha mãe (*I like my mother's apple pie*).

Now let's look at the verb gostar de used with demonstratives isto, isso or aquilo to say you *like this* or *like that*.

First, let's look at what the preposition de looks like when contracted with the demonstratives.

| | |
|---|---|
| de + este = deste *(m., sg./of this)* | de + estes = destes *(m., pl./of these)* |
| de + esse = desse *(m., sg./of that)* | de + esses = desses *(m., pl./of those)* |
| de + aquele = daquele *(m., sg./of that over there)* | de + aqueles = daqueles *(m., pl./of those over there)* |
| de + esta = desta *(f., sg./of this)* | de + estas = destas *(f., pl./of these)* |
| de + essa = dessa *(f., sg./of that)* | de + essas = dessas *(f., pl./of thoset)* |
| de + aquela = daquela *(f., sg./of that over there)* | de + aquelas = daquelas *(f., pl./of those over there)* |
| de + isto = disto *(neuter/of this)* | |
| de + isso = disso *(neuter/of that)* | |
| de + aquilo = daquilo *(neuter/of that over there)* | |

Now, let's look at some examples of how to use gostar de + demonstratives.

Eu gosto deste livro.
*I like this book.*

Você gosta dessa salada?
*Do you like that salad?*

Nós não gostamos daquele novo filme.
*We didn't like that new movie.*

Vocês gostam disso?
*Do you like that?*

## ✏ Drive It Home

A. Complete the sentences with the simple present form of the verbs in parentheses.

1. Você _____ desse filme preto e branco? (gostar)

   *Do you like this black and white movie?*

2. Eu _____ ir a um jogo. (querer)

   *I want to go to a game.*

3. Ele não _____ vir a minha festa. (poder)

   *He can't come to my party.*

4. Ela _____ um livro bom. (ler)

   *She reads a good book.*

5. Eu _____ uma festa para o meu amigo. (dar)

   *I am throwing a party for my friend.*

6. Quando você _____ ao Brasil? (vir)

   *When are you coming to Brazil?*

B. Now, put the sentences above in the plural and then translate them.

1.

   _____

2.

   _____

3.

   _____

4.

_____

5.

_____

6.

_____

**ANSWER KEY**

A. 1. gosta; 2. quero; 3. pode; 4. lê; 5. dou; 6. vem

B. 1. **Vocês gostam desses filmes preto e branco?** (*Do you like these black and white movies?*) 2. **Nós queremos ir a uns jogos.** (*We want to go to some games.*) 3. **Eles não podem vir a nossas festas.** (*They can't come to our parties.*) 4. **Elas leem uns bons livros.** (*They read some good books.*) 5. **Nós damos umas festas para os nossos amigos.** (*We are throwing some parties for our friends.*) 6. **Quando vocês vêm ao Brasil?** (*When are you coming to Brazil?*)

# Parting Words

**Parabéns!** *Congratulations!* You've finished the last lesson! How did you do? By now, you should be able to:

☐ use the verb gostar de (*to like*) (Still unsure? Go back to page 161.)

☐ use some common irregular verbs (Still unsure? Go back to page 163.)

☐ use the verbs querer (*to want*) and poder (*can*) (Still unsure? Go back to page 168.)

☐ use what you've learned to talk about socializing and entertaining (Still unsure? Go back to page 172.)

Don't forget to practice and reinforce what you've learned by visiting www.livinglanguage.com/languagelab for flashcards, games, and quizzes!

# Word Recall

You have seen many regular and irregular verbs throughout this course. Let's review some of them.

Match the Portuguese verb in the first column with the English translation in the second column. Then go back to the first column and mark R for regular verb or I for irregular verb.

| | |
|---|---|
| 1. estar | a. *to introduce* |
| 2. comer | b. *to arrive* |
| 3. beber | c. *to want* |
| 4. ficar | d. *to go* |
| 5. odiar | e. *to leave* |
| 6. apresentar | f. *to read* |
| 7. fazer | g. *to hate* |
| 8. dar | h. *to stay* |
| 9. ler | i. *to have* |
| 10. ir | j. *to drink* |
| 11. chegar | k. *to be* |
| 12. partir | l. *to eat* |
| 13. ter | m. *to give* |
| 14. querer | n. *to make/to do* |
| 15. pedir | o. *to ask for* |
| 16. vir | p. *to come* |

**ANSWER KEY**
1. k, (I); 2. l, (R); 3. j, (R); 4. h, (R); 5. g, (I); 6. a, (R); 7. n, (I); 8. m, (I); 9. f, (I); 10. d, (I); 11. b, (R); 12. e, (R); 13. i, (I); 14. c, (I); 15. o, (I); 16. p, (I)

Essential Brazilian Portuguese

# Quiz 2

Now it's time for another review! Here is a final quiz testing what you've learned in Lessons 6-10. Once you've worked through it, score yourself to see how well you've done. If you find that you need to go back and review, do so before continuing on to the final section with review dialogues and comprehension questions.

A. Translate the following sentences into Portuguese.

1. *The police station is far.*

   _____

2. *Where's the bathroom?*

   _____

3. *Turn at the second traffic light.*

   _____

4. *The bank is to the left of the supermarket.*

   _____

5. *Is there a subway in the city?*

   _____

B. Below is a list of some activities Paulo has scheduled for this week. Read the sentences that follow, and decide if the sentences are true or false. Correct the sentences that are false.

| ESTA SEMANA (THIS WEEK) | | | | | | |
|---|---|---|---|---|---|---|
| SEGUNDA | TERÇA | QUARTA | QUINTA | SEXTA | SÁBADO | DOMINGO |
| 9:30 Dentista | 12:30 Almoço com Pedro | 8:00 Reunião de vendas 20:00 Cinema | 15:00 Aula de chinês | 17:45 Entrevista com jornalista | Praia | Praia |

1. Paulo vai ao dentista às nove e meia da noite na segunda-feira. _____

2. Na quarta-feira Paulo vai almoçar com o Pedro à meia-noite e meia. _____

3. Paulo tem uma reunião às oito da manhã. _____

4. Paulo vai ao cinema às oito da noite. _____

5. Paulo vai estudar chinês na quinta-feira à tarde. _____

6. Paulo tem uma entrevista com um jornalista na quinta às seis e quarenta e cinco. _____

7. Paulo vai passar o fim de semana em casa. _____

C. Choose a verb from the list below to complete the following sentences. The verbs are in the infinitive so be sure to make all appropriate changes. The translation will guide you.

fazer, escolher, ir, querer, preferir, gostar, defender

1. Eu _____ a sopa de cebolas.

   *I prefer the onion soup.*

2. Os senhores já _____?

*Have you decided?*

3. O que a senhora _____ como acompanhamento?

*What would you like to go with that?*

4. O que vocês _____ fazer no domingo?

*What are you going to do on Sunday?*

5. Advogados _____ clientes.

*Lawyers defend clients.*

6. Nós sempre _____ viagens de negócios.

*We always take business trips.*

7. O senhor _____ vir aqui, por favor?

*Could you come here, please?*

8. Ela _____ um ingresso para as dezessete ou para as dezoito?

*Does she want a ticket for 5 or 6 p.m.?*

**ANSWER KEY**
A. 1. A delegacia de polícia é longe. 2. Onde é o banheiro? 3. Vire no segundo semáforo. 4. O banco é à esquerda do supermercado. 5. Há um metrô na cidade?
B. 1. F, … nove e meia da manhã …; 2. F, … ao meio dia e meio 3. T; 4. T; 5. T; 6. F, na sexta às cinco e quarenta e cinco da tarde; 7. F, o fim de semana na praia
C. 1. prefiro; 2. escolheram; 3. gostaria; 4. vão; 5. defendem; 6. fazemos; 7. poderia; 8. quer

# How Did You Do?

Give yourself a point for every correct answer, then use the following key to determine whether or not you're ready to move on:

**0–7 points:** Go back and study the lessons again to make sure you understood everything completely. Take your time; it's not a race! Make sure you spend time reviewing the vocabulary and reading through each Grammar Builder section carefully.

**8–16 points:** If the questions you missed were in sections A or B, you may want to review the vocabulary from previous lessons again; if you missed answers mostly in section C, check the Grammar Builder sections to make sure you have your grammar basics down.

**17–20 points:** You're doing a wonderful job! You're ready to move on to the Review Dialogues!

☐☐ **points**

# Review Dialogues
*Welcome!*

Here's your chance to practice everything you've mastered in the ten lessons of *Living Language Essential Brazilian Portuguese* with these five everyday dialogues. Each dialogue is followed by comprehension questions.

Have fun!

To practice your pronunciation, don't forget to listen to the audio! As always, look for ⏵. You'll hear the dialogue in Portuguese first, then in Portuguese and English. Next, for practice, you'll do some role play by taking part in the conversation yourself!

## Dialogue 1

11A Dialogue 1 Portuguese Only (CD 3, Track 9); 11B Dialogue 1 Portuguese and English (CD 3, Track 10); 11C Dialogue 1 Role Play Exercise (CD 3, Track 11)

### NA UNIVERSIDADE
### AT THE UNIVERSITY

First, try to read (and listen to!) the whole dialogue in Portuguese. Then read and listen to the Portuguese and English together. How much did you understand? Next, take part in the role play exercise on the audio and answer the questions here in the book.

Note that there will be words and phrases in these dialogues that you haven't seen yet. This is because we want to give you the experience of a real Portuguese conversation, where you'll come upon words that you may not have heard before. You can often guess at their meaning from context in these situations. Of course, you'll see the English translations for each line here, but see how well you can do without looking at them first.

| | |
|---|---|
| Isabela: | Oi, Rafael. Você conhece a minha amiga Mariana? |
| Isabela: | *Hi Rafael. Do you know my friend Mariana?* |
| Rafael: | Não, ainda não. Muito prazer, Mariana. |
| Rafael: | *No, not yet. It's a pleasure, Mariana.* |
| Mariana: | O prazer é meu. Você tem um irmão que estuda aqui também? |
| Mariana: | *The pleasure is mine. Do you have a brother that studies here too?* |
| Rafael: | Tenho sim. Ele estuda geografia. |
| Rafael: | *Yes, I do. He studies geography.* |
| Mariana: | Como ele se chama? |
| Mariana: | *What's his name?* |
| Rafael: | O nome dele é Felipe. Você conhece o Felipe? |
| Rafael: | *His name is Felipe. Do you know Felipe?* |
| Mariana: | Claro. Nós estamos na mesma aula de geografia marítima com o professor Tomás. |
| Mariana: | *Sure. We're in the same marine geography class with Professor Tomas.* |
| Rafael: | Que coincidência! Você gosta de estudar aqui? |
| Rafael: | *What a coincidence! Do you like to study here?* |
| Mariana: | Gosto sim, mas tenho que estudar muito. Nunca tenho tempo para sair. |
| Mariana: | *Yes, I do, but I have to study a lot. I never have time to go out.* |
| Isabela: | A Mariana quer fazer um mestrado em oceanografia no Havaí. |
| Isabela: | *Mariana wants to get a Master's in Oceanography in Hawaii.* |
| Rafael: | Que legal! Boa sorte para você. Tenho que certeza que você vai conseguir. |
| Rafael: | *Cool! Good luck to you. I'm sure you'll get it.* |
| Mariana: | Obrigada. Dê lembranças minhas ao seu irmão. |
| Mariana: | *Thanks. Give my regards to your brother.* |
| Rafael: | Dou, sim. Tchau para vocês. Até mais tarde. |
| Rafael: | *I will. Bye to both of you. See you around.* |

# ✎ Dialogue 1 Practice

A. Match the phrases in column one with their translations in column two.

1. você conhece                a. *a pleasure*

2. boa sorte                   b. *give my regards*

3. ele se chama                c. *you know*

4. muito prazer                d. *cool*

5. que legal                   e. *his name is (he's called)*

6. dê lembranças minhas        f. *good luck*

7. ainda não                   g. *I'm sure*

8. tenho certeza               h. *not yet*


B. The infinitive verbs below have been used in the dialogue, most more than once. Find the verbs and copy them as they were used in the dialogue in the spaces provided below. Finally, translate the verbs. Number 6 has been done for you as an example.

1. conhecer: _____

2. ter: _____

3. estar: _____

4. gostar: _____

5. querer: _____

6. ir: vai *to go*

7. dar: _____

**ANSWER KEY**
A. 1.c; 2. f; 3. e; 4. a; 5. d; 6. b; 7. h; 8. g
B. 1. conhece, *to know*; 2. tem, tenho, *to have*; 3. estamos, *to be*; 4. gosta, gosto, *to like*; 5. quer, *to want*;
6. vai, *to go*; 7. dê, dou, *to give*

# 🔊 Dialogue 2

▶ 12A Dialogue 2 Portuguese Only (CD 3, Track 12); 12B Dialogue 2 Portuguese and English (CD 3, Track 13); 12C Dialogue 2 Role Play Exercise (CD 3, Track 14)

## UMA CASA DE PRAIA
## A BEACH HOUSE

| | |
|---|---|
| Ana: | **Alô, mãe. Sou eu, Ana.** |
| Ana: | *Hello, mother. It's me, Ana.* |
| Mãe: | **Alô, querida. Tudo bem com você, o seu marido e as crianças?** |
| Mother: | *Hello, dear. Is everything all right with you, your husband and the children?* |
| Ana: | **Sim, tudo ótimo. Tenho uma novidade para você. Nós compramos uma casa de praia!** |
| Ana: | *Yes, everything is great! I have some news for you! We bought a beach house!* |
| Mãe: | **Que maravilha! Onde é a casa?** |
| Mother: | *How wonderful! Where's the house?* |
| Ana: | **A casa fica em Ubu, no litoral do Espírito Santo.** |
| Ana: | *The house is in Ubu, on the coast of Espírito Santo.* |
| Mãe: | **Que bom! Aquela região é muito agradável. E como é? É grande?** |
| Mother: | *How nice! That region is very pleasant. And what's it like? Is it big?* |
| Ana: | **Não é muito grande, mas é muito confortável e tem um jardim enorme. Você vai adorar!** |
| Ana: | *No, it's not big, but it's very comfortable and it has an enormous garden. You'll love it!* |
| Mãe: | **É perto da praia?** |
| Mother: | *Is it close to the beach?* |
| Ana: | **Sim, nós podemos ir à praia a pé.** |
| Ana: | *Yes, we can walk to the beach.* |
| Mãe: | **As crianças estão felizes?** |

| | |
|---|---|
| *Mother:* | *Are the children happy?* |
| Ana: | **Sim, claro. A Paula tem um amigo que também tem uma casa lá perto.** |
| *Ana:* | *Yes, of course. Paula has a friend who also has a house nearby.* |
| Mãe: | **Fale mais sobre a casa.** |
| *Mother:* | *Tell me more about the house.* |
| Ana: | **Há três quartos com bons armários. Você e o papai podem vir sempre! Há uma cozinha pequena, mas ela tem janelas grandes. E o mais importante, há uma sala de estar ampla, com uma linda varanda.** |
| *Ana:* | *There are three bedrooms with good closets. You and daddy can come all the time! There's a small kitchen, but it has big windows. And most importantly, there's a large living room with a beautiful veranda.* |
| Mãe: | **Parece um sonho! Quando vai estar pronta para a primeira visita?** |
| *Mother:* | *It sounds like a dream! When is it going to be ready for a first visit?* |
| Ana: | **Nós vamos passar as férias de verão lá, já em janeiro. Vocês estão convidados.** |
| *Ana:* | *We're going to spend summer vacations there in January. You are invited.* |
| Mãe: | **Vai ser ótimo! Mal posso esperar! Vou contar para o seu pai agora mesmo.** |
| *Mother:* | *It's going to be great! I can hardly wait! I'm going to tell your father about it right away.* |

# ✎ Dialogue 2 Practice

A. Complete the table below.

| FEMININE (SINGULAR) | FEMININE (PLURAL) | MASCULINE (SINGULAR) | MASCULINE (PLURAL) | ENGLISH |
|---|---|---|---|---|
| 1. | grandes | grande | | |
| 2. linda | | | | |
| 3. | felizes | feliz | | |
| 4. | | | | *small* |
| 5. pronta | | | | |
| 6. | | | bons | |
| 7. confortável | | | | |

B. Decide whether the statements below are true or false according to the dialogue.

1. Eles vão de carro da casa nova à praia. _____

2. Os pais de Ana podem ir para a casa nova em janeiro. _____

3. O amigo da filha da Ana também tem uma casa na praia. _____

4. A casa tem três varandas. _____

5. Não há jardim na casa da praia. _____

**ANSWER KEY**
A. 1. grande/grandes, *big*; 2. lindas/lindo/lindos, *beautiful*; 3. feliz/felizes, *happy*; 4. pequena/pequenas/pequeno/pequenos; 5. prontas/pronto/prontos, *ready*; 6. boa/boas/bom, *good*; 7. confortáveis/confortável/confortáveis, *comfortable*
B. 1. F; 2. T; 3. T; 4. F; 5. F

Essential Brazilian Portuguese

# ◑ Dialogue 3

13A Dialogue 3 Portuguese Only (CD 3, Track 15); 13B Dialogue 3 Portuguese and English (CD 3, Track 16)); 13C Dialogue 3 Role Play Exercise (CD 3, Track 17)

## UMA VIAGEM DE NEGÓCIOS
## A BUSINESS TRIP

| | |
|---|---|
| Carlos: | Com licença, Sr. Souza. Eu vou fazer uma viagem de negócios para São Paulo e o nosso gerente disse que o senhor conhece muito bem a cidade e poderia me dar umas sugestões. |
| Carlos: | *Excuse me, Mr. Souza. I'm going to take a business trip to São Paulo and our manager said that you know the city very well and could give me some suggestions.* |
| Sr. Souza: | Pois não, Carlos. Sente-se, por favor. Quando você vai para São Paulo e quanto tempo você pretende* ficar lá? |
| Sr. Souza: | *Certainly, Carlos. Sit down, please. When are you going and how long do you intend on staying there?* |
| Carlos: | Eu vou na quinta-feira da próxima semana e vou ficar lá cinco dias. Onde eu devo ficar? |
| Carlos: | *I'm going next Thursday and I am going to stay there for five days. Where should I stay?* |
| Sr. Souza: | Primeiro, fique em um hotel no centro da cidade. O trânsito é horrível, mas há uma linha de metrô muito boa e vai ser mais fácil para ir e vir.** |
| Sr. Souza: | *First, stay at a hotel in the city center. Traffic is horrible, but there is a very good subway system and it's going to be easier to come and go.* |
| Carlos: | Certo, hotel no centro. Faz sentido porque o nosso escritório fica perto do centro. |
| Carlos: | *Right, a hotel downtown. That makes sense because our office is close to downtown.* |

| | |
|---|---|
| Sr. Souza: | Segundo, vá visitar a área da Avenida Paulista. Há bons restaurantes por lá e você vai encontrar ótimas lojas para fazer compras. |
| *Sr. Souza:* | *Second, go visit the Avenida Paulista area. There are good restaurants there and you're going to find great stores for shopping.* |
| Carlos: | Bem, não sei se vou ter tempo para fazer compras. Queria ir a uma churrascaria. O senhor poderia recomendar uma? |
| *Carlos:* | *Well, I don't know if I'm going to have time to go shopping. I'd like to go to a churrascaria.\*\*\* Could you recommend one?* |
| Sr. Souza: | Claro, vá à Churrascaria Brasa de Ouro. Esse restaurante é na esquina da Av. Paulista com a Rua Pamplona. É em frente ao Museu de Arte Moderna. |
| *Sr. Souza:* | *Sure, go to the Churrascaria Brasa de Ouro (Coals of Gold). That restaurant is on the corner of Paulista Avenue and Pamplona Street. It is opposite the modern art museum.* |
| Carlos: | Vale a pena visitar o museu? |
| *Carlos:* | *Is it worth visiting the museum?* |
| Sr. Souza: | Sim, com certeza. Vá também ao parque na frente do museu. É um lugar excelente para descontrair depois de um dia de trabalho. |
| *Sr. Souza:* | *Yes, certainly. Also go to the park accross from the museum. It's an excellent place to relax after a day's work.* |
| Carlos: | Sr. Souza, eu gostaria de agradecer as recomendações. O senhor conhece Porto Seguro, na Bahia? |
| *Carlos:* | *Mr. Souza, I'd like to thank you for your recommendations. Do you know Porto Seguro, in Bahia?* |
| Sr. Souza: | Não, infelizmente. Eu ouvi dizer que é um lugar fantástico. |
| *Sr. Souza:* | *No, unfortunately. I've heard it's a fantastic place.* |
| Carlos: | É realmente lindo. Eu sou de Porto Seguro. Na sua visita à cidade, vai ser a minha vez de fazer umas sugestões. |
| *Carlos:* | *It's really beautiful. I'm from Porto Seguro. When you visit the town, it's going to be my turn to make suggestions.* |

| Sr. Souza: | Combinado. Quem sabe na minha próxima viagem de férias! |
|---|---|
| Sr. Souza: | *It's a deal! Maybe I can go there on my next vacation!* |

Notes:

\* Note that the word **pretender** in Portuguese doesn't have the same meaning as *to pretend* in English. It means *to intend*.

\*\* Also note that while in English you say *come and go*, in Portuguese the expression is switched and is said **ir e vir** (*go and come*).

\*\*\* **Churrascaria** is a restaurant where the traditional Brazilian barbecue is served.

# ✎ Dialogue 3 Practice

A. Translate the following question words into English.

1. **quando** _____

2. **quanto tempo** _____

3. **onde** _____

B. Translate the following phrases into Portuguese:

1. *excuse me* _____

2. *sit down, please* _____

3. *that makes sense* _____

4. *I've heard* _____

5. *who knows* _____

6. *it's a deal* _____

C. Rewrite the following phrases in the informal:

1. o senhor _____

2. o senhor poderia _____

3. o senhor gostaria _____

4. o senhor queria _____

D. Answer the questions in Portuguese, according to the dialogue.

1. Por que o Sr. Souza recomenda o parque?

   *Why does Mr. Souza recommend the park?*

   _____

2. Onde é a churrascaria?

   *Where's the restaurant?*

   _____

3. Por que o Sr. Souza recomenda um hotel no centro?

   *Why does Mr. Souza recommend a hotel in the center?*

   _____

4. Quando Carlos vai para São Paulo?

   *When is Carlos going to São Paulo?*

   _____

5. Quanto tempo Carlos vai ficar em São Paulo?

   *How long is Carlos going to stay in São Paulo?*

   _____

6. **Por que Carlos pode recomendar lugares em Porto Seguro?**

*Why can Carlos recommend places in Porto Seguro?*

---

**ANSWER KEY**

A. 1. *when*; 2. *how long*; 3. *where*

B. 1. com licença; 2. sente-se, por favor; 3. faz sentido; 4. eu ouvi falar; 5. quem sabe; 6. combinado

C. 1. você; 2. você pode; 3. você quer; 4. você quer

D. 1. Porque é um lugar excelente para descontrair depois de um dia de trabalho. (*Because it's an excellent place to relax after a day's work.*) 2. É na esquina da Av. Paulista com a Rua Pamplona. É em frente ao Museu de Arte Moderna. (*It's on the corner of Paulista Avenue and Pamplona Street. It is opposite the modern art museum.*) 3. Há uma linha de metrô muito boa e vai ser mais fácil para ir e vir. (*There is a very good subway system and it's going to be easier to come and go.*) 4. Na quinta-feira da próxima semana. (*Next Thursday.*) 5. Cinco dias. (*Five days.*) 6. Porque ele é de lá. (*Because that's where he's from.*)

## Dialogue 4

14A Dialogue 4 Portuguese Only (CD 3, Track 18); 14B Dialogue 4 Portuguese and English (CD 3, Track 19); 14C Dialogue 4 Role Play Exercise (CD 3, Track 20)

### FAZENDO PLANOS
### MAKING PLANS

| | |
|---|---|
| Beatriz: | Oi, Paulo. Desculpe, eu estou meia hora atrasada. |
| *Beatriz:* | *Hi Paulo. Sorry, I'm half an hour late.* |
| Paulo: | Não faz mal! Este bar é muito tranquilo. Gosto de sentar aqui, ler um livro, tomar uma cerveja e esperar você. |
| *Paulo:* | *It doesn't matter. This bar is very peaceful. I like to sit here, read a book, have a beer and wait for you.* |
| Beatriz: | É bom ver você. Você está muito bem! |
| *Beatriz:* | *It's good to see you. You look very well!* |
| Paulo: | Obrigado! Você também. E depois? O que vamos fazer? Vamos a um cinema e depois jantar fora? |
| *Paulo:* | *Thank you! So do you. And later? What are we going to do? Let's go to the movies and then have dinner?* |

| Beatriz: | Boa ideia. Mas vamos primeiro jantar e depois ir ao cinema? |
| Beatriz: | *Good idea. But let's first have dinner and after that go to the movies?* |
| Paulo: | Por que? Nós sempre vamos primeiro ao cinema e depois discutimos o filme durante o jantar. |
| Paulo: | *Why? We always go to the movies first and then we discuss the film during dinner.* |
| Beatriz: | É verdade, mas geralmente o meu dia é diferente. Eu normalmente trabalho das nove da manhã ao meio dia, e depois eu tenho uma hora para almoçar. Volto ao trabalho à uma da tarde e trabalho até as cinco horas. Mas hoje não almocei porque o gerente italiano está na cidade para várias reuniões. Também é por isso que estou atrasada. |
| Beatriz: | *It's true, but usually my day is different. I normally work from 9 a.m. to noon, and then I have one hour for lunch. I go back to work at one p.m. and work until 5:00. But today I didn't have lunch because the Italian manager is in town for several meetings. That's also why I'm late.* |
| Paulo: | Então você está com muita fome! Vamos ao nosso restaurante japonês como sempre? |
| Paulo: | *So you're very hungry! Let's go to our Japanese restaurant as always?* |
| Beatriz: | Eu gostaria de experimentar aquele restaurante vegetariano novo. Aquele no shopping center, no andar de baixo do cinema. |
| Beatriz: | *I'd like to try that new vegetarian restaurant. That one in the shopping mall on the floor below the movie theater.* |
| Paulo: | Restaurante vegetariano? Você é vegetariana agora? |
| Paulo: | *Vegetarian restaurant? Are you a vegetarian now?* |
| Beatriz: | Não, não sou. Mas, você se lembra da Mariana? Ela é nossa amiga da escola. O restaurante é dela. Ela mandou um convite. Hoje é a inauguração. Vamos? |

| Beatriz: | No, I'm not. But, do you remember Mariana? She's our friend from school. The restaurant is hers. She sent an invitation. Tonight is the opening. Let's go? |
| Paulo: | **Vamos, claro! Eu adoro comida vegetariana. É muito saudável! Você acha que vai ter preço especial para amigos?** |
| Paulo: | Sure, let's go. I love vegetarian food. It's very healthy. Do you think there's going to be special prices for friends? |
| Beatriz: | **Espero que sim.** |
| Beatriz: | I hope so. |

# ✎ Dialogue 4 Practice

A. Complete the sentences according to the dialogue.

1. **Desculpe, eu estou** _____.

2. **Não faz** _____.

3. **E depois? O** _____?

4. **Esse bar é** _____.

5. **Eu adoro** _____.

6. **Você acha que vai ter** _____

    _____?

B. Complete the sentences with ser ou estar according to the dialogue. Remember to put the verb in the appropriate form.

1. **Eu** _____ **meia hora atrasada.**

    *I'm half an hour late.*

2. Este bar _____ muito tranquilo.

*This bar is very peaceful.*

3. _____ bom ver você.

*It's good to see you.*

4. Você _____ muito bem.

*You're are/look very well.*

5. Geralmente o meu dia _____ diferente.

*Generally my day is different.*

6. O gerente italiano _____ na cidade.

*The Italian manager is in town.*

7. Então você _____ com muita fome.

*So you are very hungry.*

8. Você _____ vegetariana agora?

*Are you a vegetarian now?*

9. Ela _____ nossa amiga da escola.

*She's our friend from school.*

10. O restaurante _____ dela.

*The restaurant is hers.*

**ANSWER KEY**

A. 1. meia hora atrasada; 2. mal; 3. que vamos fazer; 4. muito tranquilo; 5. comida vegetariana; 6. preço especial para amigos

B. 1. estou; 2. É; 3. é; 4.está; 5. é; 6. está; 7. está; 8. é; 9. é; 10. é

# Dialogue 5

15A Dialogue 5 Portuguese Only (CD 3, Track 21); 15B Dialogue 5 Portuguese and English (CD 3, Track 22); 15C Dialogue 5 Role Play Exercise (CD 3, Track 23)

## EM UMA LOJA
## AT A STORE

| | |
|---|---|
| Cliente: | Boa tarde. Eu gostaria de uma mala grande. |
| *Customer:* | *Good afternoon. I'd like a big suitcase.* |
| Vendedora: | Nós temos vários modelos. A senhora gostaria de uma mala com rodinhas? |
| *Salesperson:* | *We have several models. Would you like a rolling suitcase [lit. a suitcase with little wheels]?* |
| Cliente: | Sim, por favor. É mais fácil para transportar. |
| *Customer:* | *Yes, please. It's easier to transport.* |
| Vendedora: | Que cor a senhora prefere? |
| *Salesperson:* | *What color do you prefer?* |
| Cliente: | Eu prefiro cinza ou azul escuro. Eu não quero preta porque é difícil para localizar entre as outras na esteira do aeroporto. |
| *Customer:* | *I prefer gray or dark blue. I don't want black because it's difficult to find it among the others on the conveyor belt at the airport.* |
| Vendedora: | Nós temos um modelo muito bom em liquidação. A cor da mala é vermelha. A senhora gostaria de ver? |
| *Salesperson:* | *We have a very good model on sale. The color of the suitcase is red. Would you like to see it?* |
| Cliente: | Vermelha? Por que não? Assim, nunca vou confundir. |
| *Customer:* | *Red? Why not? That way I'm not going to get it mixed up.* |
| Vendedora: | Mais alguma coisa? Que tal uma mala de mão para combinar? |
| *Salesperson:* | *Anything else? How about a carry-on to match?* |
| Cliente: | Está em liquidação também? |
| *Customer:* | *Is it on sale too?* |

| | |
|---|---|
| Vendedora: | Sim, e a senhora pode escolher outra cor. Mas mala vermelha é a última moda. |
| *Salesperson:* | *Yes, and you can choose another color. But red luggage is the latest fashion.* |
| Cliente: | Está bem. Eu vou comprar as duas. Posso pagar com meu cartão de crédito? |
| *Customer:* | *All right. I'm going to buy both. Can I pay with my credit card?* |
| Vendedora: | Claro, e também podemos fazer em três vezes sem juros.* |
| *Salesperson:* | *Of course, and we can also do it in three installments with no interest.* |

Notes:

* In Brazil it is common practice for stores to sell merchandise in installment plans.

# ✎ Dialogue 5 Practice

A. Use the color in parentheses to complete the sentences below, and then translate them.

1. Uma mala de mão _____. *(red)*

2. Eles têm dois carros _____. *(blue)*

3. Use três tomates _____. *(green)*

4. A minha bolsa de praia é _____. *(amarelo)*

5. Elas preferem casacos _____. *(black)*

6. A parede de casa é _____. *(white)*

B. Translate the following phrases into English.

1. fácil para transportar _____

2. mala com rodinhas _____

3. mala de mão _____

4. esteira do aeroporto _____

5. três vezes sem juros _____

6. última moda _____

7. em liquidação _____

C. Answer True or False

1. A cliente compra uma mala. _____

2. Mala com rodinhas é mais fácil para transportar. _____

3. Uma mala vermelha é difícil de confundir. _____

4. As malas não têm preço especial. _____

5. A cliente gostaria de pagar com cheque. _____

**ANSWER KEY**
A. 1. Vermelha, *a red carry on*; 2. Azuis, *They have two blue cars.* 3. Verdes, *Use three green tomatoes.* 4. Amarela, *My beach bag is yellow.* 5. Pretos, *They prefer black coats.* 6. Branca, *The wall in the house is white.*
B. 1. *easy to transport*; 2. *rolling suitcase*; 3. *carry-on*; 4. *conveyor belt at the airport*; 5. *three installments with no interest*; 6. *latest fashion*; 7. *on sale*
C. 1. F, 2. T; 3. T; 4. F; 5. F

You've come to the end of Living Language *Essential Brazilian Portuguese*! Congratulations! We hope you've enjoyed your experience. If you purchased *Complete Brazilian Portuguese*, you can now continue on to *Intermediate Brazilian Portuguese*. And of course, feel free to go back and review any or all of *Essential Brazilian Portuguese* at any time.

# Pronunciation Guide

## 1. SIMPLE VOWELS

**a**

In a stressed position, it is "open," as in *ah* or *father*. In unstressed positions and in the case of the article a and its plural, as (*the*), it tends to be more "closed," like the final *a* in *America* (this is particularly true in Portugal and in general with unstressed final a).

**e**

"Open" e is as in *best*; é has this sound. "Closed" e is between the sound of *a* in *case* and e in **fez**; ê has this sound, as does nasal e. Variations occur in different areas. In a final unstressed position, in Brazil, it varies between the sound of *i* in *did* and the *i* in *machine*; in Portugal, it is often clipped sharply, like a mute *e*, or it is dropped. Stressed e before **j, ch, lh,** or **nh** in Portugal can have the sound of the final *a* in *America* or of closed *e*. In an unstressed position, it is sometimes pronounced like *e* in *be* in parts of Brazil, as mute *e* in Portugal, or like *i* in *did* in both Portugal and Brazil.

**i**

Like *i* in *machine*.

**o**

"Open" o is like *o* in *off*; ó has this sound. "Closed" o is as in *rose*; ô has this sound, and so does nasal o. In an unstressed position and in the case of the definite article o, os (*the*), it is also pronounced like *oo* in *boot*.

**u**

Approximates *u* in *rule*.

## 2. VOWEL COMBINATIONS

| ai | *ai* as in *aisle* |
|---|---|

Essential Brazilian Portuguese

| au | *ou* as in *out* |
|----|------------------|
| ei | *ey* as in *they* |
| éi | similar to open *e* |
| eu | *ey* of *they* plus *u* of *lute* |
| éu | similar but with open *e* |
| ia | *ya* as in *yard* |
| ié | *ye* as in *yes* |
| ie | similar but with closed *e* |
| io | *yo* as in *yoke* |
| iu | *e* plus *u* of *lute* |
| oi | *oy* as in *boy* |
| ói | similar but with open *o* |
| ou | *ou* as in *soul* |
| ua | *wah,* like *ua* in *quadrangle* |
| ué | *we* as in *wet* |
| ui | *we* (if main stress is on *u*, however, like *u* of *lute* plus *e*) |
| uo | *wo* as in *woe,* or as *uó* |

## 3. CONSONANTS

Those consonants not mentioned are approximately like English.

| c | Before *a*, *o*, and *u*, and before another consonant, like *c* in *cut.* |
|---|---|
| c | Before *e* and *i*, like *c* in *center.* |
| ch | Like *ch* in *machine.* |
| d | As *d* in *dog* but before *e* or *i* it approximates the *j* in *just.* |

| g | Before *e* and *i*, somewhat like *s* in *measure*. |
|---|---|
| g | Otherwise, like *g* in *go*. |
| h | Not pronounced. |
| j | Like a soft *j* (see *g*, above). |
| l | Formed with the tongue forward, with the tip of the tongue near the upper teeth. |
| l | In final position is quite soft, similar to –*w*. |
| lh | Like *lli* in *million*. |
| m | In initial position in a word or syllable, like English *m*; in final position in a syllable or word, it tends to nasalize the preceding vowel; this nasal quality is especially strong in Brazil, but it may be more subtle or even absent in Continental Portuguese. (Lips should not be closed when pronouncing m at the end of a word.) |
| n | In initial position, like English *n*; in word or syllable final positions, same as for *m*, above. |
| nh | Like *ni* in *onion*. |
| qu | Before *a* or *o*, like *qu* in *quota*. |
| qu | Before *e* or *i*, usually like *k*. |
| qu | Before *e* or *i*, like *qu* in *quota*. |

| | |
|---|---|
| r | Pronounced by tapping the tip of the tongue against the gum ridge behind the upper teeth; initial r and rr are trilled with the tongue vibrating in this position. This pronunciation is heard in Portugal. In Brazil, r is pronounced at the back of the mouth (similar to a French back *r);* initial r is pronounced like a cross between *h* and German *ch,* with some variation by region. |
| s | Between vowels, *z,* like *s* in *rose.* |
| s | Before a voiced consonant (a consonant sound produced with a vibration of the cords: *b, d, ge, gi, j, l, m, n, r, v, z),* tends to be like *z* in *azure.* |
| s | Before a voiceless consonant (a consonant sound produced without a vibration of the vocal cords: hard *c,* hard *g, f, p, qu, t)* and in the final position, like *s* in *see* in São Paulo and like *sh* in *shine* in Portugal and by *cariocas* and other Northerners in Brazil. |
| s | In initial position, or after a consonant, like *s* in *see.* |
| ss | Like *ss* in *passage.* |

| t | Much like English *t*; before *e* or *i*, it is pronounced very forcefully by some *cariocas*, being palatalized and approximating the *ch* in *church*. |
|---|---|
| x | Like *z* in some words (exame), like *sh* in some words (caixa), like *s* in *see* in some words (máximo), and like *x* in *wax* in some words (táxi). |
| z | Generally, like *z* in *zeal*. However, in final position or before a voiceless consonant, *s* is also heard in Brazil; *sh* is the common pronunciation in Portugal and in a few parts of Brazil, and before a voiced consonant, it is like *z* in *azure* in Portugal. |

## 4. STRESS

Words ending in –a, –e, or –o (or in one of these vowels and –s, –m, or –ns) are stressed on the next-to-last syllable.

| casa | *house* |
|---|---|
| estudante | *student* |
| jovem | *young* |

Words ending in a nasal vowel or diphthong (two vowels pronounced in union) are stressed on the last syllable.

| papel | *paper* |
|---|---|
| manhã | *morning* |
| descansei | *I rested* |

Words not following the above rules have a written accent mark that indicates the stressed syllable.

| café | coffee |
|------|--------|
| América | America |
| Itália | Italy |
| difícil | difficult |
| órfão | orphan |

# Grammar Summary

## 1. THE DEFINITE ARTICLE

|           | SINGULAR | PLURAL |
|-----------|----------|--------|
| *Masculine* | o | os |
| *Feminine*  | a | as |

| o menino   | *the boy*  |
|------------|------------|
| a menina   | *the girl* |
| os meninos | *the boys* |
| as meninas | *the girls* |

## 2. THE INDEFINITE ARTICLE

|           | SINGULAR | PLURAL |
|-----------|----------|--------|
| *Masculine* | um  | uns  |
| *Feminine*  | uma | umas |

| um homem     | *a man*            |
|--------------|--------------------|
| uma mulher   | *a woman*          |
| uns homens   | *some (a few) men* |
| umas mulheres | *some (a few) women* |

## 3. CONTRACTIONS

Contractions of **de** with the definite article (o/a and its other forms):

| de + o = do<br>de + a = da   | de + os = dos<br>de + as = das   | *of the, from the* |
|------------------------------|----------------------------------|--------------------|
| a + o = ao<br>a + a = à       | a + os = aos<br>a + as = às      | *to the*           |
| em + o = no<br>em + a = na    | em + os = nos<br>em + as = nas   | *in the, on the*   |

| | | |
|---|---|---|
| por + o = pelo<br>por + a = pela | por + os = pelos<br>por + as = pelas | *by, through the* |

| | | |
|---|---|---|
| do menino | dos meninos | *the boy's, the boys'* |
| da menina | das meninas | *the girl's, the girls'* |
| ao menino | aos meninos | *to the boy, to the boys* |
| à menina | às meninas | *to the girl, to the girls* |
| no lago | nos lagos | *in (on) the lake, in (on) the lakes* |
| na pátria | nas pátrias | *in the homeland, in the homelands* |
| pelo menino | pelos meninos | *by the boy, by the boys* |
| pela praça | pelas praças | *through the square, through the squares* |

Contractions of de and em with the indefinite article (um and its other forms) are optional, both contracted and non–contracted forms being used.

| | |
|---|---|
| **de um artigo** or **dum artigo** | *of an article* |
| **de uma árvore** or **duma árvore** | *of a tree* |
| **em umas aldeias** or **numas aldeias** | *in some villages* |

Por never makes contractions with indefinite articles.

De and em combine with the demonstrative forms.

| | |
|---|---|
| daquela | *of that one* |
| naquele | *in that one* |

The preposition a combines with the initial a of the demonstratives aquele, etc., and with the definite article a.

| | |
|---|---|
| àquela | *to that one* |

| | |
|---|---|
| à baía | to the bay |

## 4. GENDER

Nouns referring to males are masculine; nouns referring to females are feminine.

| | | | |
|---|---|---|---|
| o pai | the father | a mãe | the mother |
| o filho | the son | a filha | the daughter |
| o homem | the man | a mulher | the woman |
| o leão | the lion | a leoa | the lioness |

The masculine plural of certain nouns can include both genders.

| | |
|---|---|
| os pais | the parents, the father and mother |
| os irmãos | the brothers, the brother and sister, the brothers and sisters |

Masculine nouns:

Nouns ending in diphthongs (vowel combinations pronounced together), –m (but not –em), –s, and –o are usually masculine.

| | |
|---|---|
| o grau | the degree |
| o elogio | the praise |
| o dom | the gift |
| o lápis | the pencil |
| um abraço | an embrace, a hug |

Names of months, seas, rivers, mountains, and letters of the alphabet are generally masculine.

| | |
|---|---|
| Janeiro é o primeiro mês. | January is the first month. |
| o Atlântico | the Atlantic |
| o Amazonas | the Amazon (River) |

| o dê | the d |
|------|-------|

Feminine nouns

Nouns ending in –a, –ie, –em, –ade, –ede, and –ice are usually feminine.

| a boca | the mouth |
|--------|-----------|
| a ordem | the order |
| a amizade | friendship |
| a parede | the wall |
| a velhice | old age |

Common exceptions:

| o homem | the man |
|---------|---------|
| a avó | the grandmother |

A good number of words ending in –a (or –ma), especially words of Greek origin, are masculine.

| o programa | the program |
|------------|-------------|
| o problema | the problem |
| o cinema | the cinema |
| o drama | the drama |
| o clima | the climate |
| o dia | the day |
| o mapa | the map |
| o idioma | the language |

–a is added to some masculine nouns ending in –r to form the feminine.

| leitor | reader | leitora |
|--------|--------|---------|
| diretor | director | diretora |

| orador | speaker, orator | oradora |
|---|---|---|

Names of islands and continents are usually feminine.

| a Europa | Europe |
|---|---|
| a Sicília | Sicily |
| a América | America |

## 5. THE PLURAL

Nouns ending in a vowel (including nasal vowels) or in a diphthong usually add –s to form the plural.

| um ato | one act | dois atos | two acts |
|---|---|---|---|
| a maçã | the apple | as maçãs | the apples |
| a lei | the law | as leis | the laws |

Words ending in –ão form the plural with –ões.

| a ambição | ambition | as ambições | ambitions |
|---|---|---|---|
| o avião | airplane | os aviões | airplanes |
| a posição | position | as posições | positions |

However, there are a few exceptions to the above rule, and these words should be learned individually. Some change –ão to –ães in the plural.

| o capitão | os capitães | the captain(s) |
|---|---|---|
| o alemão | os alemães | the German(s) |
| o pão | os pães | the bread(s) |
| o cão | os cães | the dog(s) |

Others form the plural by just adding an –s.

| o irmão | os irmãos | brother(s) |
|---|---|---|
| a mão | as mãos | hand(s) |

| o cidadão | os cidadãos | *citizen(s)* |
|-----------|-------------|--------------|
| o órfão | os órfãos | *orphan(s)* |
| o grão | os grãos | *grain(s)* |

Words that end in –m change the m into n before adding –s. This change has no effect on the pronunciation.

| o homem | *man* | os homens | *men* |
|---------|-------|-----------|-------|
| o fim | *end* | os fins | *end* |
| jovem | *young* | jovens | *young (adj.)* |
| bom | *good* | bons | *good (adj.)* |

Words ending in –r, –z, and –s add –es.

| o doutor | *doctor* | os doutores | *doctors* |
|----------|----------|-------------|-----------|
| a luz | *light* | as luzes | *lights* |
| o mês | *month* | os meses | *months* |

Words ending in unstressed –s retain the same form in the plural.

| o ônibus (o autocarro) | os ônibus | *the bus(es)* |
|------------------------|-----------|---------------|
| o lápis | os lápis | *the pencil(s)* |
| o campus | os campus | *the campus(es)* |
| simples | simples | *simple (adj.)* |

Words ending in –l drop the l and add –is. Note that the endings –éis and –óis bear a written accent.

| a capital | as capitais | *capital(s)* |
|-----------|-------------|--------------|
| o jornal | os jornais | *newspaper(s)* |
| o papel | os papéis | *paper(s)* |
| o hotel | os hotéis | *hotel(s)* |
| espanhol | espanhóis | *Spanish (adj.)* |

| azul | azuis | blue (adj.) |
|------|-------|-------------|

Words ending in –il drop the l and add –s.

| o barril | os barris | barrel(s) |
|----------|-----------|-----------|
| civil | civis | civil (adj.) |

But a few words ending in unstressed –il or –vel have irregular plurals that end in –eis.

| fácil | fáceis | easy (adj.) |
|-------|--------|-------------|
| difícil | difíceis | difficult (adj.) |
| útil | úteis | useful (adj.) |
| fútil | fúteis | futile (adj.) |
| horrível | horríveis | horrible (adj.) |
| detestável | detestáveis | dislikeable (adj.) |

## 6. POSSESSION

Possession is shown with the preposition de (of).

| o neto de Dona Maria | Dona Maria's grandson |
|----------------------|------------------------|

Possessive adjectives and pronouns agree in number and gender with the object possessed. The possessive adjective usually comes before the word it modifies.

| meu livro | my book |
|-----------|---------|
| meus livros | my books |
| minha sobrinha | my niece |
| minhas sobrinhas | my nieces |

Essential Brazilian Portuguese

In conversation, seu tends to refer to the person spoken to and can be translated as *your*. However, seu can also be used to mean *his, her*, or *their*. For greater clarity, the prepositional form with de may be used.

| | |
|---|---|
| Eles falaram de seu amigo. | *They spoke of your (his, her, their) friend.* |
| Eles falaram do amigo dele/do amigo dela/do amigo deles/do amigo delas. | *They spoke of his friend/of her friend/of their friend.* |

## 7. ADJECTIVES

Adjectives agree with the nouns they modify in gender and number.

| | |
|---|---|
| um menino alto | *a tall boy* |
| uma menina alta | *a tall girl* |
| dois meninos altos | *two tall boys* |
| duas meninas altas | *two tall girls* |

The feminine is formed with the ending –a instead of the –o of the masculine form.

| MASCULINE | FEMININE | |
|---|---|---|
| antigo | antiga | *old, ancient* |
| rico | rica | *rich* |
| baixo | baixa | *short, low* |

If the masculine form ends in –u, the feminine form ends in –a.

| MASCULINE | FEMININE | |
|---|---|---|
| nu | nua | *nude, bare* |
| mau | má | *bad* |

There is no change between genders if the masculine form ends in –e.

| MASCULINE | FEMININE | |
|---|---|---|
| contente | contente | *happy, content* |

Common exceptions:

| | | |
|---|---|---|
| este | esta | *this* |
| aquele | aquela | *that* |

The feminine ending –ã is substituted for the –ão of the masculine form.

| MASCULINE | FEMININE | |
|---|---|---|
| alemão | alemã | *German* |
| cristão | cristã | *Christian* |

With augmentatives, –ona replaces –ão.

| | | |
|---|---|---|
| bonitão | bonitona | *handsome, pretty* |

Adjectives ending in a consonant tend to have the same form for the masculine and the feminine.

| MASCULINE | FEMININE | |
|---|---|---|
| capaz | capaz | *capable* |
| comum | comum | *common* |
| formidável | formidável | *formidable* |
| simples | simples | *simple* |

| | |
|---|---|
| Ela não é capaz de fazê–lo. | *She is not able to do it.* |
| A lição é muito simples. | *The lesson is quite simple.* |

With adjectives of nationality, –a is usually added to the masculine form.

| | | |
|---|---|---|
| francês | francesa | *French* |
| português | portuguesa | *Portuguese* |

**Santo** is used before names beginning with a vowel and before **Gral**, and **São** is used before most other names; **Santa** is used before feminine names.

| | |
|---|---|
| Santo Antônio | *Saint Anthony* |
| o Santo Gral | *the Holy Grail* |

Essential Brazilian Portuguese

| São Paulo | Saint Paul |
| --- | --- |
| São Francisco | Saint Francis |
| Santa Bárbara | Saint Barbara |

## 8. COMPARISON

Regular comparison is formed with mais (*more*) or menos (*less*). The definite article produces the superlative (*most* or *least*).

| fácil | easy |
| --- | --- |
| mais fácil | easier |
| menos fácil | less easy |
| o mais fácil | the easiest |
| o menos fácil | the least easy |

Que is used to mean *than*.

| O português é mais fácil que o inglês. | Portuguese is easier than English. |
| --- | --- |

To give an equal comparison, tão … quanto … is used.

| Ela fala português tão bem quanto ele. | She speaks Portuguese as well as he does. |
| --- | --- |

With equal comparisons of nouns, tanto agrees in gender and number.

| Este teatro não tem tantas entradas quanto aquele. | This theater does not have as many entrances as that one. |
| --- | --- |

Before numerals, mais de and menos de are used.

| Eles têm mais de duzentas vacas. | They have more than two hundred cows. |
| --- | --- |

## 9. PRONOUNS

### Subject pronouns

| SINGULAR | |
|---|---|
| eu | *I* |
| tu | *you (infml.)* |
| ele | *he* |
| ela | *she* |
| o senhor | *you (m., fml.)* |
| a senhora | *you (f., fml.)* |
| você | *you (infml.)* |

| PLURAL | |
|---|---|
| nós | *we* |
| vós | *you* |
| eles | *they (m.)* |
| elas | *they (f.)* |
| os senhores | *you (m., fml.)* |
| as senhoras | *you (f., fml.)* |
| vocês | *you (infml.)* |

| PRONOUNS USED AFTER PREPOSITIONS | |
|---|---|
| para mim | *for me* |
| para ti | *for you (infml.)* |
| para ele | *for him* |
| para ela | *for her* |
| para o senhor | *for you (m., fml.)* |
| para a senhora | *for you (f., fml.)* |
| para você | *for you (infml.)* |
| para nós | *for us* |
| para vós | *for you* |

Essential Brazilian Portuguese

| PRONOUNS USED AFTER PREPOSITIONS | |
|---|---|
| para eles | *for them (m.)* |
| para elas | *for them (f.)* |
| para os senhores | *for you (m., fml.)* |
| para as senhoras | *for you (f., fml.)* |
| para vocês | *for you (infml.)* |

| DIRECT OBJECT PRONOUNS | |
|---|---|
| me | *me* |
| te | *you (infml.)* |
| o | *him* |
| a | *her* |
| o | *you (m., fml.)* |
| a | *you (f., fml.)* |
| nos | *us* |
| vos | *you* |
| os | *them (m.)* |
| as | *them (f.)* |
| os | *you (m., fml.)* |
| as | *you (f., fml.)* |

| INDIRECT OBJECT PRONOUNS | |
|---|---|
| me | *to me* |
| te | *to you (infml.)* |
| lhe | *to him, to her, to you (fml.)* |
| nos | *to us* |
| vos | *to you* |
| lhes | *to them (m. and f.), to you (fml.)* |

| REFLEXIVE PRONOUNS | |
|---|---|
| me | *myself* |
| te | *yourself (infml.)* |
| se | *himself, herself, yourself (fml.)* |
| nos | *ourselves* |
| vos | *yourselves* |
| se | *themselves, yourselves (fml.)* |

Relative pronouns

| **Ela disse que viria mais tarde.** | *She said she would come later.* |
|---|---|
| **Ele não é o homem que falou comigo ontem.** | *He is not the man who spoke to me yesterday.* |

## 10. QUESTION WORDS

| **Quê?, O quê?, Que é que … ?** | *What?* |
|---|---|
| **Que disse ele?/Que é que ele disse?** | *What did he say?* |

| **Por quê?** | *Why?* |
|---|---|
| **Por que ela não chegou antes das nove?** | *Why didn't she arrive before nine?* |

| **Como?** | *How?* |
|---|---|
| **Como se diz em português?** | *How do you say (it) in Portuguese?* |

| **Quanto?/Quanta?** | *How much?* |
|---|---|
| **Quanto dinheiro temos?** | *How much money do we have?* |
| **Quantas irmãs João tem?** | *How many sisters does João have?* |

| **Qual?/Quais?** | *Which?/What?* |
|---|---|
| **Qual é o seu?** | *Which one is yours?* |

| Quais são os seus? | Which ones are yours? |
|---|---|

| Quem? | Who? |
|---|---|
| Quem veio com ela? | Who came with her? |

| Onde? | Where? |
|---|---|
| Onde estão os livros? | Where are the books? |

| Quando? | When? |
|---|---|
| Quando aconteceu? | When did it happen? |

## 11. ADVERBS

Some Portuguese adverbs are formed by adding –mente (–ly) to the feminine singular form of the adjective.

| exclusivamente | exclusively |
|---|---|

## 12. DEMONSTRATIVES

Demonstrative adjectives

| MASCULINE | FEMININE | |
|---|---|---|
| este | esta | this |
| esse | essa | that |
| aquele | aquela | that (farther removed) |
| estes | estas | these |
| esses | essas | those |
| aqueles | aquelas | those (farther removed) |

Demonstrative pronouns

| Não quero este sem aquele. | I don't want this one without that one. |
|---|---|

There are also some neuter forms.

| isto | this, this (one) |
|---|---|
| isso | that, that (one) (near person spoken to, or mentioned by that person) |
| aquilo | that, that (one) (farther removed) |

# VERB CHARTS

## falar
*to speak*

| Present | | Imperative | |
|---|---|---|---|
| falo | falamos | | falemos! |
| fala | falam | fale! | falem! |
| fala | falam | fale! | falem! |

| Preterite | | Imperfect | |
|---|---|---|---|
| falei | falamos | falava | falávamos |
| falou | falaram | falava | falavam |
| falou | falaram | falava | falavam |

| Future | | Conditional | |
|---|---|---|---|
| falarei | falaremos | falaria | falaríamos |
| falará | falarão | falaria | falariam |
| falará | falarão | falaria | falariam |

| Future Perfect | | Past Conditional | |
|---|---|---|---|
| terei falado | teremos falado | teria falado | teríamos falado |
| terá falado | terão falado | teria falado | teriam falado |
| terá falado | terão falado | teria falado | teriam falado |

| Past Perfect | | Present Subjunctive | |
|---|---|---|---|
| tinha falado | tínhamos falado | fale | falemos |
| tinha falado | tinham falado | fale | falem |
| tinha falado | tinham falado | fale | falem |

# comer
## to eat

| eu | nós |
|---|---|
| você | vocês |
| ele / ela | eles / elas |

| Present | | Imperative | |
|---|---|---|---|
| como | comemos | | comamos! |
| come | comem | coma! | comam! |
| come | comem | coma! | comam! |

| Preterite | | Imperfect | |
|---|---|---|---|
| comi | comcmos | comia | comíamos |
| comeu | comeram | comia | comiam |
| comeu | comeram | comia | comiam |

| Future | | Conditional | |
|---|---|---|---|
| comerei | comeremos | comeria | comeríamos |
| comerá | comerão | comeria | comeriam |
| comerá | comerão | comeria | comeriam |

| Future Perfect | | Past Conditional | |
|---|---|---|---|
| terei comido | teremos comido | teria comido | teríamos comido |
| terá comido | terão comido | teria comido | teriam comido |
| terá comido | terão comido | teria comido | teriam comido |

| Past Perfect | | Present Subjunctive | |
|---|---|---|---|
| tinha comido | tínhamos comido | coma | comamos |
| tinha comido | tinham comido | coma | comam |
| tinha comido | tinham comido | coma | comam |

Essential Brazilian Portuguese

# partir
## *to depart/to leave*

| eu | nós |
|---|---|
| você | vocês |
| ele / ela | eles / elas |

| Present | | Imperative | |
|---|---|---|---|
| parto | partimos | | partamos! |
| parte | partem | parta! | partam! |
| parte | partem | parta! | partam! |

| Preterite | | Imperfect | |
|---|---|---|---|
| parti | partimos | partia | partíamos |
| partiu | partiram | partia | partiam |
| partiu | partiram | partia | partiam |

| Future | | Conditional | |
|---|---|---|---|
| partirei | partiremos | partiria | partiríamos |
| partirá | partirão | partiria | partiriam |
| partirá | partirão | partiria | partiriam |

| Future Perfect | | Past Conditional | |
|---|---|---|---|
| terei partido | teremos partido | teria partido | teríamos partido |
| terá partido | terão partido | teria partido | teriam partido |
| terá partido | terão partido | teria partido | teriam partido |

| Past Perfect | | Present Subjunctive | |
|---|---|---|---|
| tinha partido | tínhamos partido | parta | partamos |
| tinha partido | tinham partido | parta | partam |
| tinha partido | tinham partido | parta | partam |

## ser
### *to be*

| eu | nós |
|---|---|
| você | vocês |
| ele / ela | eles / elas |

| Present | | Imperative | |
|---|---|---|---|
| sou | somos | | sejamos! |
| é | são | seja! | sejam! |
| é | são | seja! | sejam! |

| Preterite | | Imperfect | |
|---|---|---|---|
| fui | fomos | era | éramos |
| foi | foram | era | eram |
| foi | foram | era | eram |

| Future | | Conditional | |
|---|---|---|---|
| serei | seremos | seria | seríamos |
| será | serão | seria | seriam |
| será | serão | seria | seriam |

| Future Perfect | | Past Conditional | |
|---|---|---|---|
| terei sido | teremos sido | teria sido | teríamos sido |
| terá sido | terão sido | teria sido | teriam sido |
| terá sido | terão sido | teria sido | teriam sido |

| Past Perfect | | Present Subjunctive | |
|---|---|---|---|
| tinha sido | tínhamos sido | seja | sejamos |
| tinha sido | tinham sido | seja | sejam |
| tinha sido | tinham sido | seja | sejam |

## estar
*to be*

| eu | nós |
|---|---|
| você | vocês |
| ele / ela | eles / elas |

| Present | | Imperative | |
|---|---|---|---|
| estou | estamos | | estejamos! |
| está | estão | esteja! | estejam! |
| está | estão | esteja! | estejam! |

| Preterite | | Imperfect | |
|---|---|---|---|
| estive | estivemos | estava | estávamos |
| esteve | estiveram | estava | estavam |
| esteve | estiveram | estava | estavam |

| Future | | Conditional | |
|---|---|---|---|
| estarei | estaremos | estaria | estaríamos |
| estará | estarão | estaria | estariam |
| estará | estarão | estaria | estariam |

| Future Perfect | | Past Conditional | |
|---|---|---|---|
| terei estado | teremos estado | teria estado | teríamos estado |
| terá estado | terão estado | teria estado | teriam estado |
| terá estado | terão estado | teria estado | teriam estado |

| Past Perfect | | Present Subjunctive | |
|---|---|---|---|
| tinha estado | tínhamos estado | esteja | estejamos |
| tinha estado | tinham estado | esteja | estejam |
| tinha estado | tinham estado | esteja | estejam |

# ter
## *to have*

| eu | nós |
|---|---|
| você | vocês |
| ele / ela | eles / elas |

| Present | | Imperative | |
|---|---|---|---|
| tenho | temos | | tenhamos! |
| tem | têm | tenha! | tenham! |
| tem | têm | tenha! | tenham! |

| Preterite | | Imperfect | |
|---|---|---|---|
| tive | tivemos | tinha | tínhamos |
| teve | tiveram | tinha | tinham |
| teve | tiveram | tinha | tinham |

| Future | | Conditional | |
|---|---|---|---|
| terei | teremos | teria | teríamos |
| terá | terão | teria | teriam |
| terá | terão | teria | teriam |

| Future Perfect | | Past Conditional | |
|---|---|---|---|
| terei tido | teremos tido | teria tido | teríamos tido |
| terá tido | terão tido | teria tido | teriam tido |
| terá tido | terão tido | teria tido | teriam tido |

| Past Perfect | | Present Subjunctive | |
|---|---|---|---|
| tinha tido | tínhamos tido | tenha | tenhamos |
| tinha tido | tinham tido | tenha | tenham |
| tinha tido | tinham tido | tenha | tenham |

# ir
## *to go*

| eu | nós |
|---|---|
| você | vocês |
| ele / ela | eles / elas |

| Present | | Imperative | |
|---|---|---|---|
| vou | vamos | | vamos! |
| vai | vão | vá! | vão! |
| vai | vão | vá! | vão! |

| Preterite | | Imperfect | |
|---|---|---|---|
| fui | fomos | ia | íamos |
| foi | foram | ia | iam |
| foi | foram | ia | iam |

| Future | | Conditional | |
|---|---|---|---|
| irei | iremos | iria | iríamos |
| irá | irão | iria | iriam |
| irá | irão | iria | iriam |

| Future Perfect | | Past Conditional | |
|---|---|---|---|
| terei ido | teremos ido | teria ido | teríamos ido |
| terá ido | terão ido | teria ido | teriam ido |
| terá ido | terão ido | teria ido | teriam ido |

| Past Perfect | | Present Subjunctive | |
|---|---|---|---|
| tinha ido | tínhamos ido | vá | vamos |
| tinha ido | tinham ido | vá | vão |
| tinha ido | tinham ido | vá | vão |